Syntactic Abilities in Normal and Dyslexic Children

Syntactic Abilities in Normal and Dyslexic Children

Susan Ann Vogel

Associate Professor
Head, Department of Education
Barat College

University Park Press
Baltimore · London · Tokyo

To Manfred

UNIVERSITY PARK PRESS
International Publishers in Science and Medicine
Chamber of Commerce Building
Baltimore, Maryland 21202

Typeset by The Composing Room of Michigan, Inc.

Printed in the United States of America by Universal Lithographers, Inc.

Library of Congress Cataloging in Publication Data
Vogel, Susan Ann.
  Syntactic abilities in normal and dyslexic children.

  1. Dyslexia. 2. Reading—Ability testing. 3. Children—Language. I. Title. [DNLM: 1. Dyslexia—In
infancy and childhood. 2. Reading. 3. Language development. WL340 V879s]
RJ496.A5V64   618.9'28'553075   75-20054
ISBN 0-8391-0818-4

Contents

Tables vii
Figures viii
Acknowledgments ix
Preface x

1. The Problem and Review of the Literature   **1**

The Causes of Reading Disability 1
Dyslexia: A Definition 2
Dyslexia and Language 3
Syntax: A Definition 5
Syntax and Reading 6
The Problem 13
Summary 13

2. Methods and Procedures   **15**

Measurement of Abilities 15
Administration and Scoring 27
Summary 30

3. The Sample   **31**

Criteria for All Subjects 32
Specific Criteria for Dyslexic and Normal Groups 38
Specific Procedures for Selection of the Sample 40
Summary 42

4. Results and Discussion   **43**

Statistical Procedures 43
Reliability of Instruments Used 44
Syntactic Abilities of Normal and Dyslexic Children 47
Functions Related to Syntax 49
Factor Analysis of Syntax and Related Functions 60
Identifying Children with Syntactic Deficiencies 68
Syntactic Ability and Reading Comprehension 73

5. Summary and Conclusions   77

The Findings 78
Implications of the Findings 81
Implications for Further Research 83
Conclusions 84

References   85

Computer Programs 94

APPENDIX A. Test of Recognition of Melody Pattern 97
APPENDIX B. Test of Recognition of Grammaticality 99
APPENDIX C. Sentence Repetition Test 101
APPENDIX D. Vogel's Scoring Key for the Berry-Talbott
             Language Test, Comprehension of Grammar 103
APPENDIX E. Vogel's Revised Scoring Key for the Berry-Talbott
             Language Test, Comprehension of Grammar 105
APPENDIX F. Oral Cloze Tests 107
APPENDIX G. Letter Distributed to Parents 109
APPENDIX H. Occupational Rating Scale for School District 65 . 111
APPENDIX I. Two-Way Analysis of Variance for Hoyt
             Reliability 113

Index   116

Tables

1. Summary of Measures Used 16
2. Means and Standard Deviations of Age, PPVT Raw Scores, and Parents' Occupations for the Sample Groups and Repeaters . . 33
3. Occupational Ratings for the Sample Groups and Repeaters . . . 36
4. Test of Significance between the Sample Groups on Age and Occupation 37
5. Univariate F Test of Significance between the Two Sample Groups on Age and Occupation 37
6. Analysis of Variance between the sample Groups on the PPVT . . 37
7. Means and Standard Deviations for Raw Scores on the Gates-MacGinitie Reading Tests, Primary B, Comprehension, and Primary CS, Speed and Accuracy, for the Sample Groups and Repeaters 39
8. Grand Means, Standard Deviations, and Reliability Coefficients. 45
9. Means, Standard Deviations, and Ranges of Syntactic Measures. 47
10. Means and Standard Deviations for All Subjects in the Two Sample Groups in Comparison to Available Normative Data . . 48
11. Test of Significance between the Two Sample Groups on the Nine Syntactic Measures 49
12. Univariate F Tests of Significance between the Two Sample Groups on the Syntactic Measures 50
13. Test of Significance for the Within-Cells Regression for the PPVT on the Syntactic Measures 51
14. Means, Standard Deviations, and Ranges of Auditory Memory for Digits and Auditory Memory for Words 51
15. Test of Significance for the Within-Cells Regression for Auditory Memory for Digits and Auditory Memory for Words on the Syntactic Measures 52
16. Univariate F Tests of Significance for Within-Cells Regression on the Syntactic Measures with Two Covariates: Auditory Memory for Digits and Auditory Memory for Words 52
17. Raw Regression Coefficients for the Syntactic Measures with Two Covariates: Auditory Memory for Digits and Auditory Memory for Words 53

18. Test of Significance between the Sample Groups on the Syntactic Measures with Auditory Memory for Digits and Auditory Memory for Words as the Covariates 53

19. Univariate F Tests of Significance between the Sample Groups on the Syntactic Measures with Auditory Memory for Digits and Auditory Memory for Words as the Covariates 54

20. Within-Cells Correlation Matrix for Factor Analysis of the Syntactic Measures, the Auditory Measures, and the Receptive Vocabulary Measure 61

21. Eigenvalues and Percentage of Communality over Six Factors . . 62

22. Rotated Factor Matrix for the Factor Analysis of the Nine Syntactic Measures, the Two Auditory Memory Measures, and the Receptive Vocabulary Measure 63

23. Loadings of the Six Factor Patterns 63

24. Raos V Statistic for the Three Best Discriminators among the Syntactic Measures 69

25. Membership Probabilities for Group Centroids under the Three-Variable Discriminant Function 70

26. Means and Ranges for Subscores of the Berry-Talbott Test . . . 71

27. R^2 of Reading Comprehension with the Three Predictors 74

28. Proportion of the Variance Unique to Each of the Three Predictors 74

Figures

1. Distribution of raw scores for the sample groups and repeaters on the Gates-MacGinitie Reading Tests, Primary B, Comprehension, and Primary CS, Speed and Accuracy 39

2. Histogram of the number of normal and dyslexic children scoring 1 SD or more below the mean 49

3. Histogram of the distributions of discriminant scores for the sample groups based on the three most discriminating syntactic measures 70

Acknowledgments

Many individuals have been instrumental in helping me in the formulation and execution of this study.

I wish to express my heartfelt thanks to Dr. Harold J. McGrady, who most unselfishly shared with me his time, knowledge, and experience. I am also grateful to Dr. Janet W. Lerner and Dr. Doris J. Johnson, who gave many insightful suggestions. To Dr. Helmer R. Myklebust and Dr. Johnson I am greatly indebted for help in generating the theoretical framework for this study.

Special thanks are due the several individuals who assisted in devising some of the experimental measures: Dr. Rae A. Moses of Northwestern University and Dr. John R. Bormuth of The University of Chicago provided their expertise in the construction of the Sentence Repetition Test and the Oral Cloze procedure; Mrs. Laura L. Lee of Northwestern University shared her insights regarding the development of syntax and permitted me to use the Developmental Sentence Scoring Procedure (at that time an experimental measure); Dr. Mildred F. Berry, formerly of Rockford College, granted me permission to use the Berry-Talbott Language Test: Comprehension of Grammar; and finally, my children, Evan and Henry, who helped by allowing me to try out many of the experimental tests on them.

Thanks are also due the many persons in School District 65, Evanston, Illinois. This particularly includes Dr. Ida Lalor, Research Director, and the principals, teachers, and staffs of the eleven elementary schools from which the subjects of this study were drawn. Finally, I am grateful to the parents and especially the children who cooperated in this study.

Preface

This study compares the oral syntactic abilities of good and poor readers. Good readers were defined as those having no reading comprehension difficulties for their age and grade levels. Dyslexic children constituted the group of poor readers. Dyslexia was defined as an inability to learn to read in the usual manner and at the expected age because of central nervous dysfunction. From a large school district of fourteen elementary schools, only twenty children met the specific criterion for inclusion in the dyslexic group.

Members of the sample groups were carefully selected to preclude the possibility of differences in syntax caused by factors such as sex, socioeconomic status, or language differences. Semantic and auditory memory factors were controlled and analyzed statistically. The major finding was that the dyslexic children were significantly inferior to the good readers in syntactic abilities.

Because of the paucity of standardized tests for assessing syntactic abilities, many of the measures employed were experimental or devised for this study. Two of the interesting peripheral findings were: the implications for devising a theoretical construct of subdivisions within the concept of syntax, and the identification of potentially useful syntactic measures as diagnostic or screening instruments.

Another area of concern was the relationship among reading comprehension and syntactic, semantic, and decoding abilities in the sample groups. These findings should interest those concerned with psycholinguistic models of the reading process.

Although this research is primarily concerned with subtle oral language deficits accompanying dyslexia, it will interest experts in reading, preschool and primary school teachers, as well as psycholinguists, speech pathologists, and learning disabilities diagnosticians and teachers.

Chapter One

The Problem
and Review
of the Literature

A person who cannot read is seriously handicapped. The ability to read is critically important for one's physical safety, for success in learning at school, and for achieving economic independence. Throughout a person's lifetime reading enhances experiential, emotional, and intellectual growth.

However, approximately eight million children, or 15 per cent of the total school-age population, are reading one or more years below age or grade norms. These children are potentially handicapped by their reading disability (United States Office of Health, Education and Welfare, 1969). According to Harris (1970) and Rabinovitch (1959), one out of ten children is unable to read at the level of his capabilities. The magnitude of the problem and the importance of literacy in our society today have helped to focus the attention of many experts from diverse fields on the problem of reading disability.

THE CAUSES OF READING DISABILITY

There are many causative factors involved in reading disability. These factors may be operative either singly or in a cluster in any one child. They have been divided into four types by Weiner and Cromer (1967): (1) The first type is a disruption in learning to read as a result of emotional conflict. Between 1935 and 1955 most reading problems were attributed to emotional disturbances, and psychotherapy was the preferred treatment (Harris, 1968). (2) Second is a deficiency in the child or in his education that causes a reading difficulty. Examples of deficiencies that can result in reading disability are inadequate language, experience, motivation, or opportunity for learning. (3) Since the 1960s there has been a growing awareness of the proportionately higher incidence of reading disability among economically, socially, and educationally disadvantaged children and a concern for their special needs (Barton, 1963). The most recent concern has been in the area of experiential and language differences that cause reading difficulty. In such cases there is a mismatch between the reading material and the reader's experiences, language, or dialect, including phonological, semantic, or syntactic dialectical differences. (4) Some reading difficulties are the result of a dysfunction either in the peripheral nervous system, as in most types of deafness, or in the central nervous system, as is assumed in the learning disability population.

DYSLEXIA: A DEFINITION

Within this broader framework of reading disability, dyslexia, one type of learning disability, is viewed as falling into the fourth subgroup. Thus dyslexic children comprise one subgroup within the larger population of reading disability children. Dyslexia is defined as a specific kind of reading disability resulting from neurological dysfunction. This dysfunction may be caused by a developmental, constitutional, or pathological anomaly, or a combination of the above (Critchley, 1964; de Hirsch, Jansky, and Langford, 1966; Hallgren, 1950; Hermann, 1959; Johnson and Myklebust, 1967). Research evidence supporting the above definition reported by Myklebust and Boshes (1969), Johnson and Myklebust (1965), and Zigmond (1966) showed that in a significant proportion of dyslexics there is demonstrable central nervous system dysfunction.

Abrams (1968) described three different types of neurological dysfunction in cases of severe reading disability. The first was diffuse brain damage; the second was specific lesion in the occipital-parietal area of the cerebral cortex; and the third was a disturbed pattern of neurological organization without definite damage. However, as in many cases of mental retardation, there may be no observable evidence of central nervous system dysfunction in certain individual cases. Therefore, Bateman (1965) stated that although learning disabilities are the result of central nervous system dysfunction which may or may not be demonstrable, evidence of neurological dysfunction is not essential for diagnostic purposes.

DYSLEXIA AND LANGUAGE

Dyslexia was originally identified and studied in an aphasiological context as a loss or impairment in an individual's ability to read. A defect in acquiring skill in reading, originally called congenital word blindness, was first described at the end of the nineteenth century and beginning of the twentieth century by Hinshelwood (1917), a British ophthalmologist. His contribution was to identify a type of dyslexia which he thought was caused by agenesis or a developmental defect in the angular gyrus of the cerebral cortex, rather than by insult to the brain. In his case studies he pointed out the absence of any general intellectual or nonlinguistic defects.

In his classic work, Orton (1937) broadened the concept of developmental disorders to include not only reading, but writing and speech problems as well. Unlike Hinshelwood, he did not believe that these disorders resulted from structural defects in the brain, but rather from physiological ones. He believed that there was some delay or deviation in the process of establishing unilateral brain superiority. He also noted that there was a hereditary factor involved in some cases. More recently, Orton's wife (1957) described the often accompanying auditory and visual processing deficits of some dyslexics. In the auditory channel she included delays or defects in other language areas, such as vocabulary, spoken language, and comprehension of language (Bender, 1958; de Hirsch et al., 1966; Orton, 1957). Orton himself felt that dyslexics were experiencing a developmental lag in acquiring all language skills, which reflected his view that all language functions were interrelated.

Myklebust (1964, 1965) and McGrady (1968) elaborated on the interrelatedness of language functions within the framework of a hierarchy of language development. In this view of language development there is a hierarchy progressing from inner language (meaningful experiences), auditory receptive language (comprehension of spoken language), auditory expressive language (oral language), written receptive language (reading comprehension), and finally to written expressive language (composition). Not only has it been found that a deficiency at any one rung in the ladder affects all subsequent development, but there is a reciprocal effect of a specific type of language functioning on all others, in which one depresses, reinforces, or enhances the others (McGrady, 1964, and personal communication, 1970).

An underlying deficit in verbal functioning such as that suggested by Orton (1937) has been further delineated by Johnson and Myklebust (1965). These authors described three subgroups within the dyslexic population. In the first subgroup were those dyslexics with visual processing disturbances. Out of 60 dyslexics in this study, slightly less than half (26) were experiencing reading difficulties resulting from visual processing difficulties. The second and larger group (of 34) was described as having auditory processing difficulties often accompanied by language deficiencies. Fourteen had needed speech therapy, six had a history of speech and language problems, and 14 had minor syntactic and word-finding difficulties. Within the second subgroup was a third type of dyslexic for whom the associational aspects of learning to read, i.e., visual-to-auditory association and vice versa, were the most troublesome.

A similar division of dyslexics into three subgroups was suggested by Doehring (1968), Ingram and Reid (1956), and Ingram (1960). The first group was characterized by immaturity in visual perceptual tasks, by reversals in letters and words, by directional confusion and poor lateralization, and by a Verbal Intelligence Quotient (IQ) on the Wechsler Intelligence Scale for Children (WISC) that was higher than the Performance IQ. The second group was made up of dyslexics with secondary speech and language disorders. These dyslexics were characterized by articulation defects and slow language development in both speaking and understanding in early childhood and in school, by a word-blending deficiency, and by a Performance IQ on the WISC that was higher than the Verbal IQ. The third group of dyslexics, which included the most severely dyslexic children, was characterized by deficits in both the auditory and visual modalities.

Kinsbourne and Warrington (1966) studied two groups of disabled readers. One group was composed of boys whose Performance IQ's were 20 or more points lower than their Verbal IQ's on the WISC. This group was characterized by symptoms remarkably similar to Gerstmann's Syndrome on tests of finger discrimination, arithmetic, and right-left orientation. In the second group the Verbal IQ's were 20 or more points lower than the Performance IQ's. This group had secondary difficulties in verbal comprehension and expression similar to aphasia.

Rabinovitch (1959, 1962) described a dyslexic population that was similar to Kinsbourne and Warrington's second group, since he included only those whose Verbal IQ's were lower than their Performance IQ's. Rabinovitch and Ingram (1968) later described these deficits as name-finding difficulties, imprecise articulation, and primitive syntax.

Hallgren (1950) also associated inadequate or immature syntax with dyslexia. He based this observation on his study of familial or genetically determined dyslexia.

Zangwill (1962) took issue with Hallgren. He described two sub-groups within the dyslexic population and associated each with different etiologies. The first subgroup was made up of the pure "visual" dyslexic and was genetically determined. The second group was characterized by language retardation caused by defective maturation of the asymmetrical functions in the two hemispheres of the brain. One aspect of language development that Zangwill pinpointed as being immature was syntax.

SYNTAX: A DEFINITION

Syntax refers to that body of rules which governs the way words are arranged into sentences. Most of the recent studies that have focused on how a child learns to combine words to form grammatically acceptable sentences have been influenced by Chomsky's theory of transformational-generative grammar (Chomsky, 1957, 1965). This theory hypothesizes that there is an innate rational ability in man which allows him to generate the underlying rules or syntax of his language once he has been sufficiently exposed to it. These rules are referred to as deep structures that are transformed to surface structures while being given phonological and semantic "flesh."

For Menyuk as well as for Chomsky, the grammar of a language is made up of phonological, semantic, and syntactic rules (Menyuk, 1969). The present study was an attempt to describe systematically one aspect of a child's grammar, namely the syntax. Included in the concept of syntax is morphology (Emig, 1965). Morphology is the study of the smallest units of meaning called morphemes, which are either free or bound. Berko (1958) found evidence that children learn a set of morphological rules, in addition to phonological, semantic, and syntactic rules, which enables them to inflect words, even those they may never have heard spoken. These rules are based on the most consistent and regular features of the English language which children have internalized as a set of rules gradually approximating adult rules. Although the burden of any message in English is conveyed mainly by the word order of a sentence, inflections provide semantic information (number and tense) and grammatical information (marking words as members of form classes). Therefore, in this study the concept of syntax includes morphology.

SYNTAX AND READING

Reading experts have typically included adequacy of vocabulary as a prerequisite for success in learning to read (Anderson, Dearborn, and Fairbanks, 1937; Betts, 1954; Schonell, 1952; Vernon, 1958). More recently they have been alerted to the importance of syntax in both receptive and expressive language (Bougere, 1969; Harris, 1970; Loban, 1969; Monroe and Rogers, 1964). On the basis of an analysis of oral reading errors, clues revealing the reading process itself have led to a new theory of reading influenced in many ways by information processing theory. This theory has provided the impetus for attempts to quantify the relative importance of syntax in reading.

According to this theory reading is considered a psycholinguistic process in which the reader possesses various amounts of three basic kinds of information: graphophonic, semantic, and syntactic (Goodman, 1970b; Lerner, 1969, 1971; Venezky and Calfee, 1970; Wardhaugh, 1969). In the reading process the child draws on his own stores of information while reacting to the printed page. He does not attend to all the details before him on the page, but selectively attends to only a sampling of them. (This model, however, does not apply to those who sound out words letter by letter or syllable by syllable.) The details that he selects are called cues because the reader uses them as a basis for making a guess as to the correct response. Goodman (1970b), in fact, refers to reading as a psycholinguistic guessing game in which the reader selects the cues and then predicts the message. The more efficient the reader is, the fewer the number of cues necessary for him to make the correct responses. The degree of efficiency a reader develops is directly related to the degree of competence the child has acquired in each of the three basic kinds of information. All responses, whether correct or incorrect, are produced by the same process. Therefore, Goodman (1969a) refers to errors as miscues and suggests that they occur in almost all reading (oral and silent), even in mature, proficient readers. Analysis of an individual's miscues reveals his linguistic competence as well as his word recognition and word attack skills. To aid in this analysis Goodman (1969*a*) has devised a taxonomy consisting of 28 classifications, nine of which are distinct types of syntactic miscues.

Based on a psycholinguistic model of the reading process, many pertinent studies have attempted to determine the contribution of each type of information and the interrelationships among the types. Ruddell (1966, 1968) found that the child's control of morphology and syntax correlated significantly with his reading comprehension and vocabulary. He reported that reading comprehension was significantly enhanced in first and second graders when emphasis was given to meaning relationships between key structural elements within and between sentences.

Syntactic Errors in Oral Reading

An analysis of 8,000 oral reading substitution errors made by 100 five-year-old boys and girls was performed by Clay (1968). She found that 72 per cent of the errors of substitution were syntactically acceptable and interpreted this finding to indicate that syntactic structure was a significant source of reading errors. Since only 41 per cent of the errors were based on visual characteristics of letters, she concluded that error behavior was guided most often by the syntactic framework of sentences, rather than by the phoneme-grapheme correspondence.

In a similar study done with first-grade children, oral reading errors were analyzed for grammatical acceptability (Weber, 1970). In the total population 91 per cent of the errors were grammatically appropriate to the preceding context, implying that even beginning readers bring their knowledge of grammatical structure to bear on their performance. This was also interpreted to mean that the reader expects sentences he reads to conform to the rules of his oral language.

The reading process has been described as a match between the syntax of the written material with that of the reader's auditory language (Beaver, 1968). In the case of a mismatch the reader alters the written material to correspond with his own syntactic system. Beaver found that 80 per cent of the oral reading errors made by second and third graders were syntactic alterations.

The importance of syntactic information in the reading process has been indirectly estimated by an analysis of oral reading errors. By these estimates approximately 80 per cent of the oral reading errors were grammatically appropriate to the preceding context.

Syntactic Complexity and Reading

The notion of syntactic complexity is a very difficult one because there is no consensus on its definition. It has been described as being reflected by measures of length, frequency counts, or transformational complexity. In most studies syntactic complexity correlates with reading comprehension difficulty.

However, Yetta Goodman's study (described in Goodman, 1970b) showed the paradoxical effect of increased syntactic complexity on reading comprehension in first graders. In this study she presented beginning readers with two stories and then tested them on comprehension. One story was written in a language style similar to that used in preprimer and primer books. The second was written in more fully formed language (with greater syntactic complexity). She found the readers' comprehension improved on the second story. She interpreted her findings as indicating that although beginners need and use more visual information than skilled readers, they begin to sample and draw on syntactic and semantic information. She showed that when the reading material is syntactically complex language, it allows the child to use graphic cues more effectively.

Strickland's (1962) study provided a tool for exploring the relationship between reading comprehension and syntactic complexity in a new way. She devised a method of describing grammatical patterns of independent clauses by assigning a symbol to each of the major phrase constituents. She then sampled, coded, and classified oral language of elementary school children. With the availability of this information on which structures occur most frequently, it was hypothesized that the more frequently a pattern was heard and spoken, the greater the ease of understanding, i.e., that frequency was related to comprehensibility. Implied in this notion of frequency is that it also correlates with syntactic complexity, i.e., that the less frequently used patterns are the more complex ones.

Ruddell (1965b) extended this hypothesis to comprehension of written material. He presented two versions of a passage to fourth-grade children. One was written with high-frequency patterns and one with low-frequency patterns of language structure. When he compared the students' reading comprehension scores on the two passages, he found that the reading comprehension scores on the passage written in high-frequency patterns were significantly higher than the comprehension scores on the passage written in low-frequency patterns of language structure. Apparently, the material written in high-frequency patterns was easier to comprehend and to remember than that written in low-frequency patterns. Ruddell interpreted these findings as indicating that reading comprehension is a function of the similarity of the patterns of the language structure in the reading material to oral patterns of language structure used by children. Miller (1962) has provided evidence in support of this finding. He explained the facilitating role of the understanding of sentence structure as an enhancement of the child's ability to narrow down the number of alternative word meanings, thus facilitating comprehension.

Tatham (1970) replicated Ruddell's (1965b) study based on Strickland's (1962) work in a population of 300 second- and fourth-grade children. The passages and tests were controlled for vocabulary and content as well as sentence structure. Her findings confirmed and extended those of Ruddell. She found that the fourth graders did better than the second graders on both tests, but that the difference in performance on the two tests was greater for the second graders. Both groups of children also had significantly better comprehension of the passage written in high-frequency patterns. Both these studies imply that knowledge of sentence structure is related to reading comprehension and that children benefit from controlled sentence structure in that it enhances reading comprehension.

In an effort to further describe the nature of syntactic complexity and its relation to reading comprehension difficulty, Bormuth (1968a) compared three measures of grammatical complexity in order to determine the size of the correlation between comprehension difficulty and each measure. The most widely accepted measure of sentence complexity until the 1960s was based on the number of words or syllables per sentence. Flesch (1948) found correlations of .66 and .48 of these measures with reading difficulty. But Chall (1967) pointed out that even though this formula has validity correlations of .5 to .7, there remains considerable variability that is not accounted for by sentence length.

Certainly the longer a sentence is, the more complex it is likely to be (Brinton and Danielson, 1958; Coleman, 1962; Stolurow and Newman, 1959). But it has been shown that sentence length and syntactic complexity do not necessarily vary in a linear fashion (Bar-Hillel, 1964). In addition, there are difficulties in manipulating sentence length as a variable. First, redundancy increases as sentence length is decreased, thus introducing an additional factor. The redundancy of syntactic elements of language structure has a positive correlation with reading comprehension (Ruddell, 1965b). Also, when sentence length is increased additional parts of speech and transformations are used so that the effect of sentence length alone is difficult to ascertain (Rubenstein, 1968).

The three measures of grammatical complexity that Bormuth (1968a) chose to investigate were outgrowths of earlier research in the fields of readability and linguistics (Yngve, 1968; Strictland, 1962). The first measure, sentence length, was based on Bormuth's own research findings and those of Coleman (1962). The unit of length was defined as the independent clause, not the sentence, counted by letter, rather than by syllable or word. Both independent clause length and word depth correlations were significant and large enough to be useful in predicting readability for both good and poor readers.

The second measure was based on Yngve's research on word depth (1968). The word depth measure refers to the number of grammatical slots that a word may fill. While reading, the individual assigns each word to a specific slot, either as he reads or in some cases after he has read the complete sentence. This procedure allows him to determine the meaning of the word. (In the case of ambiguous sentences a word simultaneously fills two slots, and one meaning cannot be assigned.) The greater the number of possible slots, the greater the word depth, and the greater the grammatical complexity. Bormuth (1968a) computed the word depth of each word, clause, and then passage, and found that the mean word depth correlation with comprehension difficulty was .77.

The third measure, based on Strickland's work on sentence types (1962), was a measure of the frequency of the patterns used in the 20 passages. Each independent clause was analyzed to determine its structure and, on the basis of Strickland's findings, each structure received a number reflecting its frequency. Numbers were then assigned to the corresponding clauses. The lower the mean frequency of each passage, the greater the comprehension difficulty. Although the correlation was significant, Bormuth felt it was too small to be a useful measure in its present form.

In Bormuth's (1969) later report of his continuing investigation of the linguistic features of written prose and their relationship to reading comprehension difficulty, he identified three distinct syntactic complexity factors. The first was Yngve depth measures for counts of left branches, which loaded heavily on measures of syntactic length. The second was Yngve depth measures for right branches, which loaded on those variables free from effects of syntactic length. And, finally, the number of different structures and transformations used in a passage was identified and found to load on redundancy and preponderance of pronoun structures. Transformational complexity, as reflected in counts of various parts of speech, correlated with comprehension difficulty at .81 (Bormuth, 1969).

The relationship between reading comprehension difficulty and transformational complexity was also studied by Coleman (1964). He used two versions of a text which differed in that the more complex version contained nominalizations, passives, and adjectivalizations and the simpler one contained the corresponding active and declarative forms. On a multiple-choice comprehension test given to adult subjects who had read each passage once, significantly more was recalled from the transformationally less complex version.

Using a variety of constructs of syntactic complexity has provided additional evidence in support of the psycholinguistic theory of reading. Increased syntactic complexity, in most cases, increases the comprehension difficulty of written material.

Morphological Ability and Reading Achievement

In the developmental sequence of language learning, syntax precedes morphology. Ervin and Miller found that inflectional markers do not appear until after the child's third birthday, but by five most children have mastered inflectional rules for regular forms (Berko, 1961; Ervin and Miller, 1963). In studying morphological development in the child between the ages of five and eight, Chappel found that learning continues after the age of five and that performance improves year by year, especially with regard to the irregular morphemes of plural and past tense (discussed in Brittain, 1970). The pattern of mastery, in addition to progressing from regular to irregular morphemes, begins with those morphemes that involve the addition of a single sound, progresses to those that require the addition of a syllable at the end, and finally to those rules that apply to an internal vowel shift (Berko, 1958; Templin, 1957).

Brittain (1970) replicated the Berko (1958) study in first- and second-grade boys and girls and then correlated inflectional performance with reading ability. For first- and second-grade boys and girls the correlations were significant, but the second-grade correlations were significantly higher than those for the first grade (.71, which is at the p less than the .001 level of significance, as opposed to .41, which is at the p less than the .01 level of significance). This finding was interpreted as indicative of the increased number of inflected forms in second-grade reading material. In addition, it suggests that the child who by the age of seven or eight has still not mastered the morphological rules of his language may be experiencing a linguistic retardation that is hampering his progress in learning to read.

These results indicate that morphological ability is of considerable importance in learning to read because of both the semantic and grammatical information that inflections provide.

Differences in Reading Ability, and Its Relation to Syntactic Ability

An alternative approach to the study of the relation between syntax and reading is to assess some aspect of syntactic ability in groups of children who differ in their reading ability. Weber (1968) compared good with poor readers on the number of times oral reading errors that upset grammatical structure of a sentence were corrected. She found that poor readers corrected an equal number of both kinds of errors, while good readers corrected only those errors that were ungrammatical. This study indicates that poor readers utilize syntactic information less efficiently than good readers.

Cromer and Weiner (1966) administered reading tests using the cloze procedure to good and poor readers and then analyzed the readers' responses with respect to appropriateness of syntactic arrangements of words. This study was based on the hypothesis that knowledge of language structures and sequences facilitates reading. Such knowledge provides the reader with information that allows him to anticipate and limit the types of words that may occur (Weiner and Cromer, 1967). Using the cloze technique, these investigators found that the poor readers' responses were less syntactic and consensual than those of the good readers, which indicates a deficiency in the former group's knowledge of language structure.

Children with reading disability whose primary difficulty was in decoding, not in reading comprehension, were given the Illinois Test of Psycholinguistic Abilities (Hepburn, 1968; Hyatt, 1968; Kass, 1966; Kirk, McCarthy, and Kirk, 1968). The children studied were between the ages of seven and nine years and in grades two through four. In Kass' study 21 reading disability children showed a marginal deficit on the Grammatic Closure Subtest when compared with normative data. In Hyatt's (1968) follow-up study this deficit was not apparent at the end of second grade. Conflicting findings in 100 third graders who were divided into two groups on the basis of reading ability were reported by Hepburn (1968). The group of poor readers was significantly different from the good readers in grammatic closure ability.

These studies seem to indicate that one possible correlate of reading disability is a deficiency in morphological and syntactic ability.

THE PROBLEM

The purpose of the present investigation was to study syntactic abilities in the auditory language of dyslexic and normal children. The basic hypothesis was that dyslexics who have difficulty in reading comprehension are deficient in syntactic abilities in comparison to normal children. The frames of reference that consider dyslexia as a specific learning disability and reading as a psycholinguistic process provided the rationale for this study.

The principle research questions posed were:

1. Are dyslexic children significantly different from the normal population in the syntactic components of language?
2. Which measures best differentiate dyslexics with syntactic deficits from normal children?
3. What is the relationship among reading comprehension and syntactic, semantic, and decoding ability in the dyslexic and normal samples?

SUMMARY

The syntactic competence of the reader is an important factor in reading comprehension. It was hypothesized that dyslexic children are deficient in the syntactic components of language in comparison to normal children. Such a deficiency was expected to contribute to reading comprehension difficulties. Therefore, the objectives of the present investigation were (1) to determine whether such a deficiency exists, and, (2) if it does exist, to determine how best to identify the child who has such a deficiency. The ultimate goal of such research is to prevent reading comprehension difficulties through early identification of such problems and recommendations for appropriate remediation.

Chapter Two

Methods
and Procedures

The primary purpose of the present investigation was to determine whether dyslexic children are deficient in syntactic abilities in comparison to normal children. Five categories of syntactic functioning in oral language were evaluated: (1) recognition of melody pattern, (2) recognition of grammaticality, (3) comprehension of syntax, (4) sentence repetition, and (5) syntax and morphology in expressive language. In addition, certain specific abilities were selected to determine their relationship to syntactic abilities. The abilities selected were (1) reading, (2) receptive vocabulary, and (3) auditory memory for digits and single words. The rationale for the selection of these abilities and the syntactic abilities is discussed below. The tests are summarized in Table 1.

MEASUREMENT OF ABILITIES

Syntactic Abilities

Nine measures were selected or devised to assess syntactic abilities among normal and dyslexic children. The division of these measures into the five categories discussed above was based on the theory of task analysis in which channel of input, processing, and channel of output are analyzed and controlled. In all measures the channel of input was auditory, but in some cases there was nonverbal visual (pictorial) input as well. None of the syntactic measures selected required that the subject read.

Table 1. Summary of Measures Used

Test Title	Source	Score
Syntactic Abilities		
Recognition of Melody Pattern	Experimental	Raw score
Recognition of Grammaticality	Experimental	Raw score
Comprehension of Syntax	Northwestern Syntax Screening Test, Comprehension; Lee, 1969	Raw score
Sentence Repetition	Experimental	Raw score
Morphology for Nonsense Words, Comprehension of Grammar	Berry-Talbott Language Tests, Comprehension of Grammar; Berry and Talbott, 1966	Raw score
Morphology for Real Words, Grammatic Closure	Illinois Test of Psycholinguistic Abilities, Grammatic Closure; Kirk, McCarthy, and Kirk, 1968	Raw score
The Oral Cloze Procedure, Low Complexity	Experimental	Raw score
The Oral Cloze Procedure, High Complexity	Experimental	Raw score
Developmental Sentence Scoring Technique	Developmental Sentence Scoring; Lee and Canter, 1971	Mean score
Receptive Vocabulary		
Receptive Vocabulary	Peabody Picture Vocabulary Test; Dunn, 1965	Raw score
Auditory Memory		
Auditory Memory for Digits	Wechsler Intelligence Scale for Children, Digits Forward; Wechsler, 1949	Span score
Auditory Memory for Words	Detroit Tests of Learning Aptitude, Auditory Attention Span for Unrelated Words; Baker and Leland, 1959	Total reproduced

Table 1 *cont.*

Table 1 *cont.*

Test Title	Source	Score
	Reading Ability	
Comprehension	Gates-MacGinitie Reading Tests, Primary B, Comprehension; Gates and MacGinitie, 1965	Raw score
Speed and Accuracy	Gates-MacGinitie Reading Tests, Primary CS, Speed and Accuracy; Gates and MacGinitie, 1965	Raw score
Vocabulary	Gates-MacGinitie Reading Tests, Primary B, Vocabulary; Gates and MacGinitie, 1965	Raw score
Oral Reading of Single Words	Wide Range Achievement Test, Reading, Level I; Jastak and Jastak, 1965	Raw score
Oral Reading of Paragraphs	Gates-McKillop Reading Diagnostic Tests, Oral Reading; Gates and McKillop, 1962	Raw score
Oral Reading of Nonsense Words	Gates-McKillop Reading Diagnostic Tests, Recognizing and Blending Common Word Parts; Gates and McKillop, 1962	Raw score

The five categories also were thought to reflect varying levels of difficulty. In all measures that required a spoken response there was no penalty for articulatory distortions that were consistent with the child's general speech habits. Whenever possible the syntactic measures were administered in a manner that would minimize memory and semantic variables. The impossibility of completely controlling for these variables in auditory language measures is one of the limitations we recognize in the present investigation. However, the statistical analysis was helpful in our assessment of the relationships among these variables.

Recognition of melody pattern Lefevre (1964), a linguist, has emphasized the importance of internalizing the intonation pattern of one's native language for the development of syntax and for reading comprehension. He considers intonation the most important and least understood signaling system at the sentence level, and he links it closely with the perception of syntactic patterns. Written material is devoid of intonation. The reader must reimplant the melody of language by utilizing the clues that punctuation and his own oral language background provide. For both Goodman (1970*b*) and Lefevre (1964) the basic reading unit is larger than a word, and the division of the flow of language into words is in some cases arbitrarily imposed. The printed word acquires meaning as part of larger language structures, and the ability to grasp these larger units is related to the reimplanting of the intonation patterns of oral language into the written form.

In an attempt to understand better the relationships among intonation, syntactic abilities, and reading comprehension, we devised a test of recognition of two melody patterns, declarative and interrogative. Six English sentences, three statements and three questions, were rewritten in such a way that semantic clues were masked but structure words, consonant and vowel order, the number of syllables, stress, and word order were retained. These sentences were read to each child twice in the melody pattern of the original sentence. The subject was asked whether he thought the sentence was telling him something or asking a question. Before the sentences were read the child was instructed to turn his back to the examiner to preclude the possibility of his interpreting visual facial clues from the examiner. On request, or if the child hesitated, the sentences were repeated more than twice. The test is given in Appendix A.

Recognition of grammaticality   A test was devised to evaluate the child's ability to recognize correct and incorrect usage. The notion of grammaticality is based on Chomsky's theory that native speakers can recognize that a sentence is grammatically correct even if it is not meaningful (Chomsky, 1957). Coleman (1965) and Hill (1961) tested this notion and found it to be true in 86 per cent of the responses. Thus this test is an extension of Chomsky's notion. It would seem that children should be able to recognize that a sentence is grammatical (especially when it is meaningful), provided the difficulty of the syntax does not exceed their level of development. It was hypothesized that the greater the syntactic proficiency, the greater the ability to identify correct and incorrect usage in sentences of increasing complexity.

To explore this hypothesis, we devised a test modeled after the Metropolitan Achievement Tests of Language Usage, number 4, part A, at all four levels—elementary, intermediate, advanced, and high school (Durost, 1961). These tests served as a guideline for the sentence types, the ratio of correct to incorrect items, the order of presentation, and the instructions for administering the test. Twenty-four sentences were composed, eight of which were grammatically correct, based on six sentence types from each level. The sentences were randomly ordered for level of difficulty, but followed the pattern of the elementary level test for right-wrong (R-W) in the following sequence: 1R, 2W, 1R, 4W, 2R, 3W, 2R, 3W, 1R, 2W, 1R, 2W. Directions explaining that this was a listening test were read to the subject. Before each sentence was read he was instructed to listen for one particular word. If he thought that the correct word was used and the sentence sounded right, he answered "correct." If he thought that the word was incorrect and the sentence sounded wrong, he answered "incorrect." Each word and each of the 24 sentences were presented twice and repeated on request. This test yielded three scores: two subscores and a total score. The first subscore was the number of correctly formulated sentences the subject could identify, the second was the number of incorrectly formulated sentences he could identify, and the total score was the sum of the two subscores. Precise test procedures and the 24 sentences appear in Appendix B.

Comprehension of syntax   Recent studies concerning the relationship between sentence comprehension and syntax have demonstrated that sentence comprehension is dependent on the syntactic as well as the semantic aspects of language and that it varies with syntactic complexity (Chomsky, 1969; Coleman, 1964; Slobin, 1966). Based on these studies and others, including Fraser, Bellugi, and Brown's Imitation Comprehension and Production Test (ICP), Lee (1969) devised a technique of using contrasting sentence-pairs to isolate those children between the ages of three and eight who are deficient in the areas of receptive and expressive syntactic ability (Berko, 1958; Carrow, 1968; Fraser, Bellugi, and Brown, 1963; Lee, 1969, 1970; Lerea, 1958; Wolski, 1962). The receptive section of Lee's test, the Northwestern Syntax Screening Test (NSST) (Lee, 1969), which assesses the child's comprehension of syntactic forms, was used in this study. This test consists of 20 sentence-pairs, arranged in order of increasing difficulty, which are presented orally to the child. He then has to scan four pictures, two of which are decoys, and identify, one at a time, the correct two, thus exhibiting his understanding of the grammatical contrast in the sentence-pair.

Sentence repetition   Repetition of sentences is a complex task involving receptive language, syntactic ability, and memory factors

(Menyuk, 1969; Schlesinger, 1968). The difficulty of recall is directly related to syntactic complexity, according to results of analyses of sentence repetition errors, such as the study by Slobin and Welsh (reported in Ryan and Semmel, 1969) and that by Wales (reported in Schlesinger, 1968), among others (Mehler, 1963; Menyuk, 1969). The process seems to be a complex one involving comprehension, memory, and expression of language and not imitation or memory span alone.

A Sentence Repetition Test was devised consisting of 20 sentences in order of increasing syntactic complexity. Nine of the sentences were eight words in length. Eleven were nine words in length. Contractions were counted as one word. The vocabulary was controlled for level of difficulty to include words with which the child should be familiar (Thorndike, 1931). Syntactic complexity was increased in two ways: (1) developmentally, by application of the Developmental Sentence Scoring Procedure (Lee and Canter, 1971) to the construction of the sentences, and (2) transformationally, by an embedding of an increasing number of underlying sentences in each sentence (Chomsky, 1965; Jacobs and Rosenbaum, 1968). The range in developmental sentence score, reflecting the level of difficulty, was from 11 to 33. The number of underlying sentences increased from two to four: sentences 1–5 having two, 6–15 having three, and 16–20 having four underlying sentences. These sentences are listed in Appendix C.

Syntax and morphology in expressive language   The task of formulating sentences involves many prerequisites and abilities. Exposure to, and comprehension of, fully formed language are perhaps the primary prerequisites. In addition, the child must be able to manipulate symbols and generalize the underlying principles of sentence structure (Brown and Bellugi, 1964; Chomsky, 1957; Ervin, 1964; Johnson and Myklebust, 1967; Lenneberg, 1964). Five measures of syntax in expressive language were selected. In four measures the response was a single word, and in the fifth measure the response was spontaneous, connected, free-flowing language. Two of these measures assessed knowledge of morphological rules; two employed the Oral Cloze technique; and the fifth measure was an analysis of a sample of spontaneous language elicited in a specified way by the examiner. In all but the two Oral Cloze Tests the primary source of information was auditory, but there was also a nonverbal visual stimulus. In the Oral Cloze Tests the only source of information was auditory.

To measure knowledge of morphological rules, we selected two tests, one employing nonsense words, the other employing real words. In both test measures the channel of input was both auditory and visual, since a picture was presented along with an incomplete sentence. Berko devised a test using nonsense words to investigate the child's knowledge of morphological rules (Berko, 1958; Gleason, 1969). The rationale for using nonsense words rather than real words was to enable the examiner to be certain that the task required the use of morphological rules and not just exposure, memory, and imitation. A correct response indicated that the child possessed adult morphological rules. The choice of test items was based on the vocabulary of first-grade children and a frequency inventory of morphological features which was then used to rate these features as to level of difficulty. Berry's adaptation of Berko's test was used in this investigation (Berry and Talbott, 1966). The Berry-Talbott Language Test of Comprehension of Grammar was selected in preference to the Berko test because it included a greater number of complex items. Simple items were defined as those that required the addition of a single terminal phoneme, while complex items required the addition of a terminal syllable, an internal vowel shift, or the formation of a compound word. Two items using real words were deleted, leaving 36 items, of which ten were simple and 26 were complex. All 36 items were presented, and the subtotals (simple and complex) and total score were determined. The scoring guidelines used in this study are given in Appendix D. A revised scoring key (not employed in this investigation) appears in Appendix E.

To administer the Berry-Talbott Test, the examiner shows the child a card on which there are one or more pictures of one or more imaginary animals depicting the desired response. Beneath the pictures are written two sentences which the examiner then reads to the child. In the first sentence, which is complete, the imaginary animal or his action is referred to by a nonsense word (e.g., *nad, gish, fooz*). In the second sentence a word is missing, and the child has to recall the nonsense word from the first sentence and inflect it, giving an oral response. The sentences are reread to the child on request.

The second test selected was the Grammatic Closure Subtest of the Illinois Test of Psycholinguistic Abilities (Kirk, McCarthy, and Kirk, 1968). In this test the examiner describes two pictures orally, using one sentence for each picture. One sentence is complete, while in the second a word is missing and has to be remembered from the first sentence, inflected, and then supplied by the subject. The items chosen were thought to be familiar enough so that the responses would be automatic. Since the semantic elements are provided by the examiner, this test involves exposure, comprehension, memory, and the use of morphological rules.

The Oral Cloze procedure is an adaptation of the cloze readability procedure, which was designed as a measure of reading comprehension difficulty (Bormuth, 1968*b*; Rankin, 1965; Taylor, 1953). Such a test is constructed by deleting every—*n*th word, or a specific kind of word, from a passage and substituting a blank for the deleted word. The subject must then respond by filling in the blanks. Each response that is the exact word that was deleted is credited.

Rankin (1957) was the first to divide the deletions into structural and lexical words, based on the writings of Fries (1952). Rankin found a high correlation between the structural and syntactic elements of language. Similarly, he found high correlations between lexical and semantic elements. He interpreted this finding to indicate that the syntactic and semantic aspects of language could be assessed by the two different kinds of deletions.

Weaver (1961) also explored the use of structural and lexical deletions on the basis of the above evidence and from studies of semantic and syntactic aphasics (Jones and Wepman, 1961). He found that meaning is transmitted primarily by lexical elements, while structural words function as cues for lexical words and provide the plan for storage and retention. In addition, he analyzed the responses to structural-word deletions, comparing these with the exact words that had been deleted from the original passage. These responses to structural-word deletions were also compared with forms utilized in the subject's spontaneous language. Structural-word deletion responses were more similar to forms utilized in spontaneous language than to the exact words deleted from the original passage. In the case of the responses to lexical-word deletions, there was a greater similarity between the responses and the original deleted words.

In the present investigation two versions of a 110-word passage were read to each subject twice (Bormuth, 1969). The readability of the passages was suitable for grades one through five. The versions varied in transformational complexity, based on the mean number of underlying sentences (Chomsky, 1965; Jacobs and Rosenbaum, 1968). In the low transformational complexity version the mean number of underlying sentences was 3.6, in contrast to a mean of 13.0 underlying sentences in the more complex version. Because at this time there is no evidence pointing to one particular way of analyzing sentences for syntactic complexity, these sentences were analyzed in two ways: for mean number of underlying sentences and according to Menzel's classification of transformational complexity (Menzel, 1970). By the latter method the mean scores for transformational complexity of the simple and complex versions were 18.0 and 65.0, respectively.

On the average, every tenth structural word was deleted. As an adaptation of Taylor's (1956) procedure, a click followed by a pause of about four seconds was heard by the subject in place of the missing word. After hearing the entire passage read once with deletions, the subject was then encouraged to respond after listening for the second time to each phrase, the click, and the subsequent words up to the next mark of punctuation. The low complexity version of the passage was administered first, with at least three other measures administered between the first version and the second. The subjects were encouraged to guess, and on request sentences or sentence fragments were reread. The maximum number of deletions in each version was ten. The Oral Cloze Tests are presented in Appendix F.

As an analysis of a spontaneous language sample, Lee and Canter's Developmental Sentence Scoring (DSS) Procedure was used to evaluate the level of syntactic development in free-flowing speech (Lee and Canter, 1971). This procedure enables an examiner to evaluate the child's ability to use generally accepted rules of grammar in formulating correct and complete sentences. The procedure was based on a comprehensive study of the process of language acquisition in normal and deviant language development and on recent research in the field of psycholinguistics (Bloom, 1968; Brown, 1968; Brown and Fraser, 1964, 1968; Cazden, 1968; C. Chomsky, 1969; N. Chomsky, 1957, 1965; Klima and Bellugi, 1966; McNeill, 1966; Menyuk, 1969).

The Developmental Sentence Scoring Procedure is an in-depth analysis of 50 complete nonecholalic sentences. These sentences are elicited from the child in conversation with the examiner through the use of pictures and toys as stimulus materials. The sentence scoring is based on a model of syntax development that includes eight grammatical features of mature language usage. These include (1) indefinite pronouns and/or noun modifiers, (2) personal pronouns, (3) main verbs, (4) secondary verbs, (5) negatives, (6) conjunctions, (7) interrogative reversals, and (8) wh-questions. Words or structures are grouped and assigned a score not greater than 8, which reflects the degree of difficulty and the developmental sequence within each category. The scores for each of the 50 sentences are then summed. A mean score is computed, which yields the DSS.

Receptive Vocabulary

One of the important prerequisites for reading comprehension, according to research studies conducted over the past three decades, is the ability to understand the meaning of individual words, referred to here as receptive vocabulary (Anderson, Dearborn, and Fairbanks, 1937; Doehring, 1968; Hildreth, 1935; Holmes, 1954; Robinson, 1949). Deficits in receptive vocabulary in children can be the result of several factors, among which are limited intelligence, environmental deprivation, and level of education of the parents.

Within the aphasiological framework such deficits have been referred to as receptive aphasia (Johnson and Myklebust, 1967; McGrady, 1968; Myklebust, 1954; Schuell, Jenkins, and Jimenez-Parson, 1964; Wepman, 1951). Receptive aphasics may "parrot" in speaking and, similarly, may "word-call" in reading. In such cases the reading comprehension difficulty is secondary to the receptive language deficit. In order to identify and exclude from the present study children whose difficulty in reading comprehension was primarily caused by a deficit in receptive vocabulary, the Peabody Picture Vocabulary Test (PPVT) was administered. In addition, it was thought that this measure would provide valuable information pertaining to the still unresolved question of the independence or interrelatedness of semantics and syntax in language development and reading comprehension (Berry, 1969; Chomsky, 1969; Ruddell, 1968; Rystrom, 1970a, b; Schlesinger, 1968).

The PPVT consists of a series of words presented orally to the subject one at a time. The child is instructed to choose the one picture out of four that goes best with the word presented.

Auditory Memory

One of the important prerequisites for normal development of syntax is the ability to remember a series of words in the correct sequence (Johnson and Myklebust, 1967; Miller, 1967). This ability provides the individual with the opportunity to abstract and internalize the syntactic structures of the language to which he is exposed. To explore auditory memory span and its relation to syntactic abilities, we selected two measures.

Auditory memory for digits This measure was taken from the Digit Span subtest of the Wechsler Intelligence Scale for Children. The Digits Forward section of the Digit Span Subtest was administered to all subjects according to the instructions stated in the manual (Wechsler, 1949). The child is required to repeat a series of digits in the same order in which they are presented, beginning with three. The test is discontinued when the child fails on the first and second trial of any span. The score is the highest number of digits repeated without an error.

Auditory memory for words An alternative method for assessing auditory memory for meaningful material is to use nouns rather than numbers. The Auditory Attention Span for Unrelated Words Subtest from the Detroit Tests of Learning Aptitude was selected and administered according to instructions stated in the manual (Baker and Leland, 1959). This test consists of 14 lines of words in which every second line is increased by one word, beginning with two words and increasing up to an eight-word span. The score is the sum of all the words correctly repeated regardless of order.

Reading Ability

Six tests were selected to assess reading ability. These particular tests were chosen to enable us to determine the relationship between syntactic ability and reading comprehension. As discussed above, there is a growing body of literature and research that indicates a positive and high correlation between these two abilities.

Silent reading comprehension The Gates-MacGinitie Reading Tests of Comprehension, Primary B, and of Speed and Accuracy, Primary CS, were selected as measures of the child's ability to read and understand whole sentences and paragraphs (Gates and MacGinitie, 1965). As mentioned above, it was assumed that the child relies on his knowledge of syntax as one of three basic sources of information in the process of reading and comprehending paragraphs. Primary B consists of 34 paragraphs of increasing length and difficulty. Above each paragraph are four pictures. The child must mark the picture that best describes the paragraph or answers the question at the end of the story.

Speed and accuracy To determine whether difficulty in interpreting pictures was a contributory factor in a child's performance on the above test, we administered the Gates-MacGinitie Reading Test of Speed and Accuracy, Primary CS (Gates and MacGinitie, 1965). This is a test of reading comprehension of paragraphs in which there are no pictorial stimuli. It was constructed to measure the speed with which a child can read and understand sentences. How rapidly a child reads may be a function of several important variables, among which are method of instruction, efficiency of cerebral processing, strategies employed by the reader, his age and proficiency, the nature of the reading material, and, not least among them, the syntactic complexity of the written material and the reader's syntactic ability (Schlesinger, 1968). The child's task in this test is to read as many of the short paragraphs as he can within the time limit and, for each paragraph, to circle the word that best answers the question or completes the last sentence. There are 32 short paragraphs of relatively equal length and difficulty. Each paragraph is followed by four words from which the child must choose and circle one. The time limit is such that few children can complete all the paragraphs.

Vocabulary Included in the Gates-MacGinitie Reading Tests of Comprehension is a vocabulary test that samples the child's ability to recognize or analyze isolated words. This test was included because knowledge of syntax and contextual clues are not involved in the task, in contrast to the paragraph comprehension tests. The child is required to circle the one word out of four that best corresponds to the picture. There are 48 pictures, each with four words which increase in difficulty and configural similarity.

Oral reading of single words To understand the reading process more fully, we asked the child to read orally. Through this task he revealed his own particular strategies, strengths, and weaknesses. The Wide Range Achievement Test—Reading, Level I—was selected to assess the child's ability to recognize and analyze isolated words orally (Jastak and Jastak, 1965). This test consists of recognizing and naming letters at the prereading level and pronouncing 75 single words which increase in difficulty. It was selected because it assesses both the child's word recognition and work attack skills when no syntactic cues are provided. The test is discontinued when the subject makes an error on 12 consecutive words.

Oral reading of paragraphs This test is the first subtest of the Gates-McKillop Reading Diagnostic Tests and consists of seven paragraphs of increasing difficulty and length (Gates and McKillop, 1962). The subject is required to read each paragraph orally. The test is discontinued if the child makes 11 or more errors on two consecutive paragraphs. This test was included to help us determine the effect of syntactic information on word recognition and word attack skills in oral reading.

Oral reading of nonsense words To examine the relationship between word attack skills, word recognition, and reading comprehension, we chose the subtest for recognizing and blending common word parts from the Gates-McKillop Reading Diagnostic Tests (Gates and McKillop, 1962). This test is made up of 23 nonsense words which resemble real words only in that they are composed of parts of real words. This list of words is devoid of configural, semantic, and syntactic information. The child is required to analyze and pronounce new and meaningless, but phonetically consistent, "words." This task involves many underlying abilities. First, the child must be able to perceive correctly and consistently the individual letters. Second, he must be able to discriminate auditorially among all the different sounds. Third, he must be able to recall the visual symbol and associate it with its auditory equivalents as the result of spontaneous discovery and/or instruction. Fourth, he must then recall the sound that is associated with that letter, vowel, or particular combination of letters. Finally, he must be able to retain the sequence of sounds, blend them, and pronounce the "word." The absence of semantic and syntactic information in nonsense words necessitates his relying on these five abilities.

ADMINISTRATION AND SCORING

Exceptions to Standardized Procedure

Standardized directions for administering the tests were followed in all tests except the following:

1. The instructions for the Test of Recognition of Melody Pattern appear in Appendix A. After the child was given the instructions, he was asked to turn his back to the examiner. Each item was read two or more times at the child's request.

2. The directions for the Test of Recognition of Grammaticality were adapted from the Metropolitan Achievement Tests of Language Usage, number 4, part A (Durost, 1961). These instructions differed from those of the Metropolitan test in three ways. First, instead of reading the test, the child heard the sentences read orally, and he was asked to listen for one word. Second, the response of the child was oral rather than written. Finally, in this test the child was not required to correct the incorrect usage, whereas in the Metropolitan test he was (see Appendix F).

3. The directions for the Sentence Repetition Test were the same as those used in the Auditory Attention Span for Related Words Test in the Detroit Tests of Learning Aptitude (Baker and Leland, 1959).

4. The instructions for the Oral Cloze Tests were an adaptation of those suggested by Bormuth, 1969 (see Appendix G). The main difference was that in the written cloze procedure the child was instructed to read the passage silently and fill in the blanks. In the Oral Cloze Test the examiner read to the child and recorded his responses. The child listened to the passage and responded orally. A muted click signaled a deletion analagous to a blank in the written cloze. The sound of a buzzer was used by Taylor (1956). The entire passage was read with deletions at least twice. The first time the child was instructed to listen, not to respond. On the second reading each sentence or sentence-part was read with pauses at the click and again after several words beyond the click had been read. At the child's request, or if he did not respond, the sentence was reread. The child was encouraged to guess, and if he responded with a two-or-more word answer he was reminded that only one word was missing and was encouraged to guess again.

Order of Presentation

The Gates-MacGinitie Reading Tests of Comprehension, Primary B, and of Speed and Accuracy, Primary CS, were administered in a separate session to groups of children in their own schools prior to individual testing. The ratio of child to examiner did not exceed 1 to 12. Northwestern University graduate students in the field of Learning Disabilities and District 65 classroom teachers assisted the examiner in groups larger than 12. In all sessions the procedures for administering the tests prescribed in the manuals were followed (Gates-MacGinitie, 1965).

The remaining 16 measures were administered individually, and with all subjects the PPVT was administered first. The second test, the Gates-MacGinitie Reading Tests of Comprehension, Vocabulary, was selected because it provided the examiner the opportunity to score the PPVT while the subject was completing the silent vocabulary test. Twelve measures were then administered in a random order to each subject. Randomness was achieved by having the child select one envelope from a diminishing pile of 11, each of which contained a different test form, thus indicating the test order.

A twelfth envelope contained the test form for the high transformational complexity version of the Oral Cloze Test. It was thought that this test should follow the low complexity version with at least three other test measures intervening. Therefore, this envelope was not included in the original stack until this requirement had been met. The two remaining measures, the Sentence Repetition Test and the Developmental Sentence Scoring Procedure, were respectively the next to the last and the last measures administered to all subjects. The rationale for these being the seventeenth and eighteenth measures was twofold. The Developmental Sentence Scoring Procedure was to be administered after the child had warmed up to the examiner and felt comfortable in the testing situation, so as to elicit from him a representative speech sample. Second, because of the nature of the scoring procedures for these two measures, a permanent recording of the child's responses and language was made, and this necessitated changing the reel of tape. By administering both these measures consecutively and at the end of the testing session, the examiner was able to minimize the time spent on the mechanics of tape recording.

Scoring

For purposes of transcribing and accuracy of scoring, the three oral reading tests, the Sentence Repetition Test, and the Developmental Sentence Scoring Procedure were recorded on a Wollensak take recorder, model T-1500.

The scoring of standardized measures was performed according to the manual in all cases but one. In the test of auditory memory for words (Detroit Tests of Learning Aptitude, Auditory Attention Span for Unrelated Words) only the simple score was tabulated. This score was defined in the manual as the sum of all the words repeated in each of the 14 lines (Baker and Leland, 1959).

There were five measures that were experimental and one other that did not include instructions for scoring. For the five experimental measures each item was scored as either correct or incorrect, with only one correct answer for each item. These five tests were the Test of Recognition of Melody Pattern, Test of Recognition of Grammaticality, the Sentence Repetition Test, and the two Oral Cloze Tests.

Sentence Repetition Test   A response was scored as correct if the child repeated the sentence accurately without any additions, substitutions, or changes of word order. Repeating more than once, one or more words within a sentence was not considered an error. Similarly, if a word such as "it's" was repeated as "it is," or vice versa, and no other changes were made, the response was scored as correct.

Oral Cloze Tests In the case of the Oral Cloze Tests, Rankin (1959, 1965) had compared the exact-word and synonym scoring methods for the Cloze procedure and reported no significant differences in test reliability or validity. In view of these findings and the consideration that synonym scoring is both time-consuming and subjective, the exact-word method of scoring was followed in the present investigation (see Appendix F).

Berry-Talbott Language Tests: Comprehension of Grammar This is an experimental test. No scoring key was available. On the basis of the experimental findings reported by Berko in 1958 and 1961 on the morphological rules for regular and irregular inflections in English, and of an analysis of the responses of 30 college students to this test, a scoring key was devised (see Appendix D). For 33 of the 36 items there was only one correct response, while for three items there were several possible correct answers (see Appendix D).

Further analysis of over 70 adult responses has resulted in a revised scoring key (Appendix E). Reanalysis of these data, using the revised key, and a corresponding reliability check are forthcoming (Vogel, in press).

SUMMARY

Four areas of behavior were assessed in the present investigation. The first was the area of syntactic abilities, in which there were five categories assessed by nine measures. Receptive vocabulary was the second area, assessed by one test. Third, auditory memory was investigated for both digits and words. The final group of six measures assessed the area of reading ability. Table 1 lists the tests used in this investigation, their sources, and the scores they yielded.

Chapter Three

The Sample

The primary purpose of the present study was to compare the syntactic abilities in oral language of dyslexic children with those of normal children. The sample was drawn from 12 of the 16 elementary schools in Evanston, Illinois, School District 65. These 12 schools were considered to be the most heterogeneous and representative of a cross-section of the total community.

The sample consisted of two groups of 20 children each: a group of dyslexic children and a group of normal children. All dyslexic children who conformed to the criteria outlined below and for whom parental permission to participate was granted were included in the study. The normal children who were included also met the criteria given below and had received parental permission. Each normal child was matched to a dyslexic child within three months of his chronological age. Fourteen of the 20 normal children were drawn from the same school as their dyslexic matches. Of these 14 pairs, in six cases both children came from the same classroom, and in the other eight pairs they were drawn from different classrooms within the same school. The remaining six pairs were matched by chronological age but came from different schools in the district.

The criteria for inclusion in the dyslexic group were based on our definition of dyslexia. Dyslexia was viewed as a specific type of learning disability and was defined as an inability to learn to read in the usual manner and at the expected age because of central nervous system dysfunction, which is the result of developmental, constitutional, or pathological aberrations (Critchley, 1964; de Hirsch, Jansky, and Langford, 1966; Hallgren, 1950; Hermann, 1959; Johnson and Myklebust, 1967). Because the neurological dysfunction may or may not be demonstrable in each individual case, evidence of neurological dysfunction was not essential for inclusion in the dyslexic group (Bateman, 1965). However, several other conditions, in addition to the primary presenting symptom of difficulty in learning to read, had to be met. The dyslexic child is one who has normal mental abilities, sensory acuity, and emotional stability (Johnson and Myklebust, 1967). Moreover, his reading difficulty is not the result of cultural or educational inadequacies (Kirk, McCarthy, and Kirk, 1968; McGrady, 1968). Thus children who were included in the dyslexic group had a deficit in reading despite normal mental, sensory, and emotional functioning, and had not been deprived of adequate cultural and educational opportunities. The selection procedure included screening or assessment of these areas. In addition, there were certain criteria established for all children.

CRITERIA FOR ALL SUBJECTS

Age

The children ranged in age from seven years, four months to eight years, five months. This age range was selected because (1) each child would have had at least 1.5 years of instruction in reading, (2) available measures of syntactic ability were appropriate for this age, and (3) the basic morphological rules and syntactic structures have been mastered in normal children by the age of seven, although development continues beyond that age (Berko, 1961; Chomsky, 1969; Hunt, Loban, and Strickland, 1970; Lefevre, 1964; McCarthy, 1946; Monroe and Rogers, 1964; Slobin, 1966, Templin, 1957). The mean age for the two sample groups was virtually the same, 7.9 years (see Table 2).

A subgroup of six dyslexic second graders who had met every criteria other than age were tested for interpretive purposes. Each had repeated one year of school. They were neither matched with control subjects nor included in any statistical analyses other than the reliability studies. They are referred to throughout the discussion as the "repeaters."

Table 2. Means and Standard Deviations of Age, PPVT Raw Scores, and Parents' Occupations for the Sample Groups and Repeaters

Variable	Group	Mean	Standard Deviation
Age	Normal	7.93	0.31
	Dyslexic	7.94	0.33
	Repeaters	9.03	0.29
PPVT score	Normal	81.25	9.30
	Dyslexic	76.90	11.63
	Repeaters	74.67	5.54
Parent's occupation	Normal	8.15	2.47
	Dyslexic	8.55	2.49
	Repeaters	6.67	2.55

Sex

It has been reported repeatedly that in the reading disability population there are many more males than females. The ratio of males to females has varied from two to one to as high as five to one (Critchley, 1964; Eisenberg, 1966; Myklebust, 1967; Myklebust and Boshes, 1960). The reason for the higher incidence of males is not yet known, but these theorists have suggested as possible explanations a sex-linked inherited tendency, the greater vulnerability of the male sex, motivational factors, and the expectations of key people in the child's environment.

In the present investigation only males were selected in order to control for differences in syntax that may be attributable to sex differences.

Race

The linguists and psycholinguists who have directed their attention to the reading process have helped to focus the attention of reading experts on the unique reading comprehension obstacles for the dialectically different child (Goodman, 1970a; Lerner, 1969; Reed, 1969; Shuy, 1968; Weiner and Cromer, 1967). Their contributions have reawakened interest in the implications and fundamental importance of oral language for reading.

When oral language is deficient, disordered, or different from written language, it is expected that there will be a commensurate effect on the reader's comprehension of written language (Johnson and Myklebust, 1967).

A comparison of black dialect with standard English has pinpointed differences in phonology, semantics, and syntax (Bailey, 1968). The greater the dialectic differences between the reader and the written language, the greater will be the barriers to reading comprehension (Goodman, 1969b).

The oral language of the black population in District 65 is possibly syntactically different from the language the students read in their school texts or reading comprehension tests. If this is the case, then their reading comprehension difficulties may in part be the result of this difference. To avoid including children whose reading comprehension difficulties might be related to dialectic differences in syntax, we included only Caucasian children in our investigation.

Monolingual Language Background

In addition to dialectic differences in language background as a cause of reading comprehension difficulties, frequent exposure to more than one language or to English as a second language may be a handicap to reading comprehension (Harris, 1970; Hildreth, 1964; Smith, 1969). The effect of bilingualism on language development has long been a subject of great interest and controversy. As a control for the possible effects of bilingualism on reading comprehension, children who spoke, or heard members of their immediate families speak, a foreign language in their homes were excluded from this study.

Educational Experience

All subjects in both groups had attended kindergarten and first grade and were enrolled in second-grade classes or its equivalent setting in a multiage team. Children who had repeated a grade were excluded from this study, so that the subjects in the two sample groups had received the same number of years of instruction.

Emotional Adjustment

The children who participated in this study had not been referred to or evaluated by the Special Services Department of the school district because of primary emotional disturbances. Neither were any of them receiving supportive help from the school social worker or an outside agency. Some children in the dyslexic group did show mild anxiety or frustration during the reading tests as a result of their reading difficulties. These children were not eliminated since their primary difficulty was their learning disability.

Sensory Acuity and Physical Health

Both audiometric and visual screening tests were performed within the academic calendar year by the school nurse. The screening tests were administered in accordance with the regulations of the Evanston Board of Health. Audiometric screening was carried out at the 20-decibel hearing level for the frequencies 500–4000 hertz (International Standard Organization standards). The Snelling E Chart (20 or 10 feet) was used in the visual screening tests. A child was considered to have passed the visual screening test if he made no more than two errors in either eye at 20/40. All the subjects participating in this study passed both these screening measures.

School nurses' records and the family doctor's medical report required at the time of school entrance provided information regarding the school attendance record and general state of health of each child. Children who were on medication for neurological dysfunction were not excluded from this study. Only two children were known to be on medication. All subjects were in good health and had no restrictions in their daily activities while in school.

Socioeconomic Status

The detrimental effects of an environment with limited and/or monotonous stimulation on a child's language and cognitive development have been a subject of great concern to educators, psychologists, and other scholars in related fields in the recent past (Bernstein, 1961, 1964; Deutsch, 1965; Eisenberg, 1966; Harlow, 1949; Hunt, 1961). It has been noted that this kind of environment is more likely to be found in orphanages and in families of low socioeconomic status (SES) than in middle- and upper-class families. The language deficiency is often related as a causative factor to reading difficulties (Harris, 1968; Weiner and Cromer, 1967). Barton (1963) reported that while upper-middle-class children were ahead one grade level or more in reading ability by the end of first grade and in following years, lower-middle-class children were one or more years behind grade placement by fourth or fifth grade. Preventive programs and special methods for the teaching of reading and language arts are being implemented to identify and aid these children (Bereiter and Engelmann, 1966; Whipple and Black, 1966).

Because low SES can contribute to an individual's reading difficulties, no child was included in this study whose SES was in the lower one-fifth based on the father's or mother's occupation. School District 65's occupational rating scale was used in this study. It appears in Appendix H. For purposes of statistical analysis numbers were substituted for the letters A through J used by the district. Only children whose father's or mother's occupation was coded between 3 and 10 were included. The occupational ratings for the sample groups and repeaters appear in Table 3. The means and standard deviations for occupation of the sample groups and repeaters appear in Table 4. The means for the two sample groups for occupation are almost identical, but there is a two-point difference between the means of the sample groups and the repeaters. The results of the test of significance between the sample groups, with Wilks' lambda criterion used, and univariate F tests on age and occupation are reported in Tables 4 and 5. There were no significant differences between the groups in SES.

Receptive Vocabulary

One of the many reasons for difficulty in reading comprehension is inadequate receptive vocabulary. To exclude children with such difficulties from the present investigation, we administered the PPVT. The lower limit for the IQ's based on raw scores and chronological age for

Table 3. Occupational Ratings for the Sample Groups and Repeaters

Occupational Rating	Normal Group	Dyslexic Group	Repeaters
3		1	
4	2	2	1
5	2		2
6	3		
7		1	
8	1	3	2
9	1	1	
10	11	12	1

Table 4. Test of Significance[a] between the Sample Groups on Age and Occupation

F	$df\ hyp$[b]	$df\ err$[c]	p less than
0.110	2	37	.896

[a] Wilks' lambda criterion was used.
[b] Degrees of freedom-hypothesis.
[c] Degrees of freedom-error.

Form A was set at 85. No child received an IQ lower than 95. The univariate F test revealed no significant differences between the two groups. The mean raw scores, standard deviations, and univariate analysis are summarized in Tables 2 and 6.

Table 5. Univariate F Test of Significance between the Two Sample Groups on Age and Occupation

Variable	$F(1,38)$	MS[a]	p less than
Age	0.002	0.000	.969
Occupation	0.293	1.600	.591

[a] Mean square.

Intellectual Ability

An important feature that differentiates the dyslexic child from the slow learner or mentally retarded child is his level of intellectual ability. The Preschool Inventory (Caldwell, 1967) was utilized in order to determine whether a child's intelligence level was within normal limits. This measure was selected because the school district had administered

Table 6. Analysis of Variance between the Sample Groups on the PPVT

Source	SS[a]	df	MS	F	p less than
Within groups	4211.550	38	110.830	1.707	
Between groups	189.225	1	189.225		.199

[a] SS, sums of squares.

the test to all children when they entered kindergarten. It was particularly advantageous that the test was administered individually. The raw score, together with chronological age, yielded a percentile score (Caldwell, 1967). The lower limit of intelligence was set at 1 SD (standard deviation) below the mean (the 16th percentile). However, no child's score fell below the 20th percentile. Seven children had not been tested because they had transfered into the district. For six of these seven, other measures of intelligence were available: Stanford-Binet Intelligence Scale (for one); WISC (for two); the Otis-Lennon Mental Primary Test (for one); Cooperative Primary Test (for two) (*Cooperative Primary Tests,* 1967; Otis and Lennon, 1967; Terman and Merrill, 1960; Wechsler, 1949). None of these six scores was more than 1 SD below the mean. One child was new to the system in September 1970, but from teacher reports and the PPVT score there was every indication of mental ability within normal limits (Dunn, 1965).

Because of the different intelligence measures used, these scores were inappropriate for statistical analysis. The function of these tests was to serve as a gross measure to indicate adequate mental ability.

SPECIFIC CRITERIA FOR DYSLEXIC AND NORMAL GROUPS

Two standardized tests of silent reading comprehension were selected as the criteria for differentiating the dyslexic and normal groups. Silent reading comprehension was selected as preferable to a silent vocabulary test because the task enabled the reader to use three primary sources of information—graphic, semantic, and syntactic—to aid him in unlocking the words and comprehending the paragraphs. The basic hypothesis was that the internalization of morphology and the syntactic structure of one's language is an important prerequisite for sentence and paragraph comprehension in reading.

Children who met all the other general criteria were included in the dyslexic group if they scored 1 SD or more below the mean on both the Gates-MacGinitie Reading Tests, Primary B, Comprehension, and Primary CS, Speed and Accuracy (Gates and MacGinitie, 1965). Those who scored in the 50th percentile or above on these two measures, met all other criteria, and matched a dyslexic by ±3 months of his chronological age comprised the normal group. Mean reading scores and standard deviations for the sample groups and repeaters appear in Table 7. The distribution of scores is represented in Figure 1.

Table 7. Means and Standard Deviations for Raw Scores on the Gates-MacGinitie Reading Tests, Primary B, Comprehension, and Primary CS, Speed and Accuracy, for the Sample Groups and Repeaters

Reading Test	Group	Mean	Standard Deviation
Comprehension	Normal	30.75	2.92
	Dyslexic	11.75	3.37
	Repeaters	14.00	2.10
Speed and Accuracy	Normal	20.45	5.04
	Dyslexic	4.10	2.57
	Repeaters	6.00	2.61

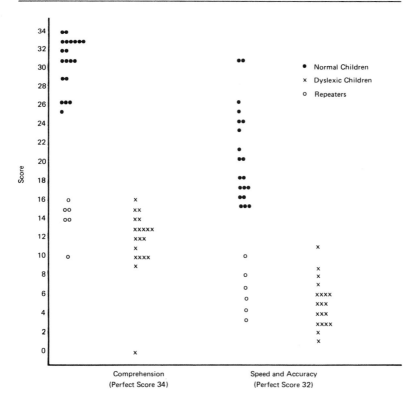

Figure 1. Distribution of raw scores for the sample groups and repeaters on the Gates-MacGinitie Reading Tests, Primary B, Comprehension, and Primary CS, Speed and Accuracy. Perfect scores were 34 on the Comprehension Test and 32 on the Speed and Accuracy Test. ●, Normal children; ×, dyslexic children; ○, repeaters.

SPECIFIC PROCEDURES FOR SELECTION OF THE SAMPLE

In October 1970 schoolwide reading achievement tests were administered to all second graders in the district (in the 12 schools there were
981 children). Half the students were given the Primary Reading Profiles, Level 1, and the remaining half, Harper and Row Second Year
Readiness Test (Stroud, Hieronymus, and McKee, 1957; Van Roekel,
1968). The comprehension subtest scores served as indicators of which
children were likely to meet the selection criteria. Information regarding age, sex, race, and SES were available from the Data Processing
Department of District 65.

The Dyslexic Group

There were 96 Caucasian males who met the criteria for the dyslexic
group in reading, grade, sex, and race. Forty of these were eliminated.
One did not meet the SES criteria, three had moved out of the district,
11 had repeated a grade, and two had entered kindergarten early and
therefore did not meet the criteria for age. Through the Special Services
Department of District 65 it was ascertained that one was deaf, one was
mentally retarded, eleven were emotionally disturbed, and four were
borderline emotionally disturbed. Through examination of cumulative
records it was found that six had foreign language backgrounds. From
the original 96 children, 56 remained. For interpretive purposes six of
the repeaters were reincluded. In addition, the four borderline emotionally disturbed children were given the group tests for silent reading
comprehension, but after consultation with the school nurse and social
worker in their respective schools, they too were eliminated.

The Normal Group

Before the two silent reading tests were administered to the potential
dyslexic subjects, a group of 76 normal second-grade children were
selected. These were children who scored at the mean or above on the
comprehension section of one of the two standard reading achievement
tests administered to all second graders in October 1970. These children
were selected because they met the criteria for reading ability, sex, race,
and grade placement. Out of these 76 children 13 were eliminated: one
was borderline emotionally disturbed, one was the child of a racially
mixed marriage, one had moved out of the school district, four had

foreign language backgrounds, and six were either repeaters or too old for inclusion.

The Selection Criteria Measures

The two selection criteria measures of silent reading comprehension of paragraphs, Gates-MacGinitie Reading Tests, Primaries B and CS, were then administered to all the remaining potential dyslexic subjects and normal subjects except one, a normal subject who was absent. These two tests were administered in a one-hour testing session in the public schools during the regular school hours, in accordance with procedures stated in the manual (Gates and MacGinitie, 1965). Twenty-nine of the potential dyslexics were less than 1 SD below the mean on one or both of these measures and therefore were excluded. Among the normal group 16 who had scored below the mean on one or both of the selection criteria were also excluded. The school nurses in each of the 12 participating schools were then consulted about the results of the visual and auditory screening tests. All 27 dyslexics and the remaining 46 normal children had passed the screening tests within the 1970–1971 academic year.

Parental Permission

Letters of explanation requesting permission to test their children individually during the school day or during spring vacation were then sent to the parents of the 27 dyslexics. On these letters, as a double check, parents were asked to indicate whether any language other than English was spoken in the home. Seven more children had to be eliminated: in three homes a second language was spoken, and for four children parental permission was not granted. This left a total of 20 in the dyslexic group (see Appendix F).

At the same time letters were sent to the parents of the 27 out of the 46 possible normal children who were closest in chronological age to the 27 dyslexic children. One child's parents did not grant permission. Of the remaining 26, the 20 normal children who were closest in chronological age to the 20 dyslexic children were then tested individually. There were ten children whose parents preferred that they be tested during the spring vacation. The remaining children were tested over a period of two months in their individual schools. Permission to test the six second graders who had repeated a grade, but had met every criteria other than age, was granted, and they were also tested individually during the same period.

SUMMARY

Each sample group consisted of 20 Caucasian males who were enrolled in second grade or its equivalent in the Evanston Public Schools, District 65. Their ages ranged from seven years, four months to eight years, five months. No child had repeated any grade or been granted special permission to enter school at a younger age than the regulations required. All the children had monolingual language backgrounds, had at least average intelligence and receptive vocabulary, and had adequate auditory and visual acuity. There were no indications of primary problems in emotional adjustment or physical health, or lack of adequate educational, social, or cultural opportunities.

Two measures of silent reading comprehension of paragraphs were administered to the sample groups. Each child in the dyslexic group had scored 1 SD or more below the mean on the two measures. The children in the normal group were selected on the basis of chronological age, and each had obtained a score at the mean or above on the same two measures. There were no significant differences between the groups in age, receptive vocabulary, or SES.

Chapter Four

Results
and Discussion

STATISTICAL PROCEDURES

1. Information pertinent to the interpretation of the results of all other statistical procedures was provided from a reliability study done on all measures. This information was of critical importance in regard to the experimental and devised measures that were used. Hoyt's procedure, which estimates internal consistency on the basis of an item analysis and an analysis of variance, was used (Hoyt, 1941).

2. As a test of the major hypothesis, i.e., dyslexic children are significantly different from normal children in syntactic abilities, a multivariate analysis of variance was considered to be the most appropriate statistical procedure (Program MANOVA). The multivariate analysis was done with the nine syntactic measures, with Wilks' lambda criterion used for level of significance for all nine measures simultaneously and the univariate F test used for each of the nine measures individually. In addition, the analysis of variance technique was used to determine whether the sample groups differed significantly on age, occupational rating, receptive vocabulary, auditory memory, and reading measures (other than the two selection criteria).

3. Two of the assumed inherent characteristics of measures of auditory language are the semantic element and the memory factor. Measures of auditory language involve the use of words. Similarly, the nature of auditory language requires that, for purposes of integration, the listener retain in proper sequence what he hears. An attempt was made to

control for semantic and memory factors in the construction and administration of the syntactic measures. Because of the impossibility of controlling completely for these factors, an indirect method, an analysis of covariance, was used to partial out that proportion of the variance resulting from these two factors, thereby increasing the precision of the measures (Winer, 1962). The criteria were the nine measures of syntax, and the covariates were the measures of receptive vocabulary (semantic factor) and of auditory memory (memory factor).

4. The answer to the second research question—What measures best differentiated the dyslexics with syntactic deficiencies from normal children?—was sought through a stepwise discriminant analysis with the nine syntactic measures (Program EIDISC). This procedure determined the relative contribution of each measure to the difference between the sample groups.

5. A multiple-regression analysis was done to enable us to determine the relationship between syntax and reading comprehension, and the interrelationships among the above two, receptive vocabulary, and decoding ability. On the basis of the information provided by this analysis, that proportion of the variance of reading comprehension attributed to the nine syntactic measures was determined. In the multiple-regression analysis the criterion was reading comprehension, whereas the composite syntax score, receptive vocabulary, and decoding ability were the predictors. In this way the relative contribution of each predictor to reading comprehension was determined (Program BMD29).

6. A factor analysis (Program BMDO3M) was done to indicate the nature of the syntactic measures. Twelve measures were used: nine syntactic measures, two auditory memory measures, and one measure of receptive vocabulary. This procedure was useful in analyzing and interpreting the experimental measures and indicating directions for future research. Following are the results of the statistical analyses.

RELIABILITY OF INSTRUMENTS USED

Because six of the measures used were experimental, and to aid in the interpretation of the results, the reliability of all measures was estimated by a two-way analysis of variance (Hoyt, 1941). According to this procedure, for every item each child's response was analyzed and compared with his responses to all other items. An estimate of internal consistency, error, and the true variance yielded a reliability coefficient, the Hoyt r. The Hoyt r is computed by subtracting the mean square of the error (MS_e) from the mean square of the individuals (MS_i), which is then divided by the mean square of the individuals. The formula is:

$$\text{Hoyt } r = \frac{MS_i - MS_e}{MS_i}$$

where MS_e is estimated from the interaction of items and individuals.

The results of the analysis of variance on all measures are presented in Appendix I. The grand means, standard deviations, and reliability coefficients for the 46 children tested (the two sample groups and the six repeaters) are given in Table 8. Whenever possible the standardization sample means, standard deviations, and reliability coefficients presented in the manual are given in parentheses.

Table 8. Grand Means, Standard Deviations, and Reliability Coefficients

Measure	Grand Mean	SD	Hoyt r
Syntactic Abilities			
Test of Recognition of Melody Pattern	4.39	1.39	.49
Test of Recognition of Grammaticality	15.70	2.62	.51
NSST	35.39 (38.2)	2.80	.59 (.75[a])
Sentence Repetition Test	13.28	4.08	.85
Berry-Talbott Test	22.46	6.22	.89
Grammatic Closure Test	26.20	3.30	.68 (.75[a])
Oral Cloze Test, Low Complexity	6.15	2.70	.78
Oral Cloze Test, High Complexity	4.46	1.81	.62
DSS	11.25	1.99	.80[b] (.83[a])
Receptive Vocabulary			
PPVT	78.50	10.17	.93 (.79[c])
Auditory Memory			
Test of Auditory Memory for Digits	6.28[d]	2.37	.82

Table 8, *cont.*

Table 8, *cont.*

Measure	Grand Mean	SD	Hoyt *r*
Test of Auditory Memory for Words	38.46 (43.0)	7.30	.71
Reading Ability			
Gates-MacGinitie Test for Comprehension	20.30 (17.2)	9.76 (7.8)	.95
Gates-MacGinitie Test for Speed and Accuracy	11.46 (14.1)	8.85 (7.1)	.96
Gates-MacGinitie Test for Vocabulary	34.43 (27.7)	10.99 (10.1)	.95
Wide Range Achievement Test, Reading	54.52 (51.48)	13.26 (12.68)	.96 (.99[e])
Gates-McKillop Test for Oral Reading	16.35	10.03	.89
Gates-McKillop Test for Recognizing and Blending Common Word Parts	9.33	7.62	.95

[a] Hoyt *r* reported by Hedberg, 1971.
[b] Gamma reliability coefficient.
[c] Pearson product-moment reliability coefficient.
[d] This is not a span score.
[e] Split-half reliability coefficient.

For the DDS, the measure of spontaneous language, the gamma reliability coefficient is reported. Gamma *r* is based on a one-way analysis of variance, which is appropriate for the DSS since it does not consist of specific items. Rather, for each of the 50 sentences that comprise the language sample there is a different stimulus question, toy, or picture. Therefore, although the formula for the gamma *r* is the same as that for the Hoyt *r*, in this case the MS_e is estimated from the variance within the individual (thus a one-way analysis of variance), rather than from the interaction of items and individuals, as in the Hoyt *r* (a two-way analysis of variance).

Guilford (1954) cautions against placing too much emphasis on the reliability coefficient of a test. He feels it is neither the most important nor the most useful information concerning a test, but rather the minimum information that should be available. With this in mind, the attempt was made in the following discussion to relate the results of the reliability study to the findings of the other analyses.

SYNTACTIC ABILITIES OF NORMAL AND DYSLEXIC CHILDREN

The nine syntactic measures were divided into five categories, as discussed in Chapter 2. The means, standard deviations, and ranges of the two sample groups and the repeaters on the nine syntactic measures are reported in Table 9. A comparison of the means of the dyslexics with the means of the repeaters reveals that for all but one measure, Test of Comprehension of Syntax (NSST), the repeaters performed more poor-

Table 9. Means, Standard Deviations, and Ranges of Syntactic Measures

Category	Measure	Group	Mean	SD	Range
Recognition of Melody Pattern	Test of Recognition of Melody Pattern	Normal	5.35	0.67	4–6
		Dyslexic	3.75	1.45	1–5
		Repeaters	3.33	1.03	2–5
Recognition of Grammaticality	Test of Recognition of Grammaticality	Normal	16.60	1.60	14–19
		Dyslexic	15.60	2.76	10–20
		Repeaters	12.83	3.06	7–15
Comprehension of Syntax	NSST	Normal	36.30	2.76	30–40
		Dyslexic	34.65	2.76	29–38
		Repeaters	35.00	2.53	31–38
Sentence Repetition	Sentence Repetition Test	Normal	15.80	2.04	13–19
		Dyslexic	12.15	3.60	7–17
		Repeaters	8.50	4.93	2–14
Syntax and Morphology in Expressive Language	Berry-Talbott Test	Normal	26.60	3.62	19–31
		Dyslexic	20.40	4.98	10–28
		Repeaters	15.50	7.77	2–23
	Grammatic Closure Test	Normal	28.55	2.11	25–32
		Dyslexic	24.75	3.04	19–33
		Repeaters	23.17	2.14	20–26
	Oral Cloze Test, Low Complexity	Normal	7.90	5.45	5–10
		Dyslexic	5.45	2.59	0–9
		Repeaters	2.83	1.17	1–4
	Oral Cloze Test High Complexity	Normal	5.60	1.10	3–7
		Dyslexic	3.85	1.87	0–7
		Repeaters	2.67	1.03	1–4
	DSS	Normal	12.40	1.63	10.66–16.12
		Dyslexic	10.59	1.86	7.08–13.66
		Repeaters	9.60	1.49	7.80–11.66

ly despite their being older and having received an additional year of schooling.

The additional year of maturation did not help these severely dyslexic repeaters to close the gap between their level of syntactic competence and that of the normal child. Despite the age difference, their mean scores were lower than those of the dyslexic nonrepeaters on all but one of the syntactic measures. Therefore, it seems that for these six repeaters the benefits of having lived a year longer, of having been exposed to language for an additional year, and of having repeated a grade have been ineffectual in bringing their syntactic abilities up to the level of competence of their younger (normal) peers.

For two of the syntactic measures normative data were available (Kirk, McCarthy and Kirk, 1968; Lee, 1969), and it was possible to compare the sample groups with the normal population. The means and standard deviations of all the subjects in the two sample groups and normative data provided in the manuals are given in Table 10. On the Grammatic Closure Test there is a discrepancy on two points between the mean score of the two sample groups of 26.65 and that of the standardization sample of 24.00 for the age seven years, eleven months. Hedberg (1971) also found a discrepancy, favoring her sample over that of the standardization sample. The reason for these discrepancies is not clear. Perhaps there is some environmental variable unique to the sample which facilitates morphological development. In addition, tallies were made of the number of normals and dyslexics in the two sample groups who scored 1 SD or more below the mean of the normal group on the syntactic measures. Two measures are represented by subscores. A histogram depicting these tallies is given in Figure 2.

To answer the first research question—Are dyslexic children significantly different in syntactic abilities from normal children?—we did a multivariate analysis of variance using the MANOVA Program. The variance between the two sample groups on all nine syntactic measures

Table 10. Means and Standard Deviations for All Subjects in the Two Sample Groups in Comparison to Available Normative Data

Measure	Source	Mean	SD
NSST	Sample groups	35.48	2.85
	Manual norms	38.20	
Grammatic Closure Test	Sample groups	26.65	3.22
	Manual norms	24.00	

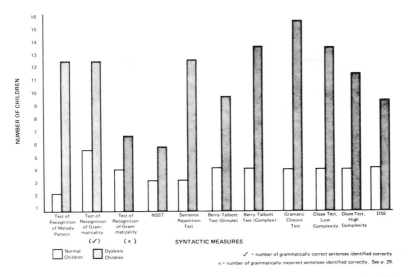

Figure 2. Histogram of the number of normal and dyslexic children scoring 1 SD or more below the mean. The shaded bars are the dyslexic children.

was significant at the .001 level of significance with Wilks' lambda criterion (Table 11). On two of the nine measures (Recognition of Grammaticality and NSST) there were no significant differences between the sample groups, while on the remaining seven the differences were at a high level of significance based on the univariate F tests. These results are reported in Table 12.

FUNCTIONS RELATED TO SYNTAX

In the construction and administration of the syntactic measures, semantic and memory factors were minimized (see Chapter 2). Because of the nature of the measures and the impossibility of controlling

Table 11. Test of Significance[a] between the Two Sample Groups on the Nine Syntactic Measures

F	$df\ hyp$	$df\ err$	p[b] less than
4.849	9	30	.001[b]

[a] Wilks' lambda criterion was used.
[b] p less than the .001 level of significance.

Table 12. Univariate F Tests of Significance between the Two Sample Groups on the Syntactic Measures

Measure	$F(1,38)$	MS	p less than
Test of Recognition of Melody Pattern	20.141	25.600	.001[a]
Test of Recognition of Grammaticality	1.963	10.000	.169
NSST	3.583	27.225	.066
Sentence Repetition Test	16.002	136.900	.001[a]
Berry-Talbott Test	20.299	384.400	.001[a]
Grammatic Closure Test	21.048	144.400	.001[a]
Oral Cloze Test, Low Complexity	13.204	60.025	.001[a]
Oral Cloze Test, High Complexity	13.025	30.625	.001[a]
DSS	10.640	81,450.625	.002[b]

[a] p less than the .001 level of significance.
[b] p less than the .01 level of significance.

completely for these variables, an analysis of covariance was done. The purpose of this procedure was to increase the precision of the syntactic measures by partialling out that proportion of the variance resulting from semantic and auditory factors.

Receptive Vocabulary

The means and standard deviations for the PPVT, a measure of receptive vocabulary, are reported in Table 2. The two sample groups did not differ significantly on this measure, as can be seen from the analysis of variance in Table 6. There was a considerable discrepancy between the mean of 79.08 for the sample groups when compared with the mean of 65.81 for the standardization sample for the age range seven years, six months to eight years, five months (Dunn, 1965). Our sample mean was approximately 1.5 SD above the standardization sample mean, as can be seen in Table 8. The reason for this discrepancy is not clear, but it may be that there is a significant difference between the environment and SES of the subjects in this study and those of the standardization sample. A similar discrepancy was also reported by Hedberg (1971), favoring a sample drawn from the Evanston community.

An analysis of covariance was employed with the nine measures of syntax as criteria and the PPVT as a single covariate. This was to determine whether there was significant regression of semantic elements on the nine syntactic measures. With the use of Wilks' lambda criterion it was found that there was no significant regression resulting from semantic elements (Table 13). Therefore the effect of receptive vocabulary as a covariate on the nine syntactic measures was disregarded.

Auditory Memory

A second analysis of covariance was done with two auditory memory measures (digits and words) as covariates. The means, standard deviations, and ranges of the two auditory memory measures for all subjects are reported in Table 14. The analysis of covariance revealed significant regression at the .001 level of significance with Wilks' lambda criterion (Table 15). Univariate F tests showed that there were significant regression effects on three of the nine syntactic measures: Sentence Repetition; Cloze, Low Complexity; and Cloze, High Complexity. Table 16 summarizes these results.

The raw regression coefficients for the nine syntactic measures, as determined by this analysis of covariance, appear in Table 17. On the basis of these coefficients, corrected raw scores were computed for each individual. When that portion of the variance resulting from the effects of auditory memory was partialled out, the difference between the sample groups on the nine syntactic measures was at the .017 level of significance with Wilks' lambda criterion (Table 18). While on the

Table 13. Test of Significance[a] for the Within-Cells Regression for the PPVT on the Syntactic Measures

F	$df\ hyp$	$df\ err$	p less than
1.54	9	29	.180

[a] Wilks' lambda criterion was used.

Table 14. Means, Standard Deviations, and Ranges of Auditory Memory for Digits and Auditory Memory for Words

Measure	Group	Mean	SD	Range
Test of Auditory Memory for Digits	Normal	7.65	1.87	4–7
	Dyslexic	5.50	2.40	3–7
	Repeaters	4.33	1.03	4–5
Test of Auditory Memory for Words	Normal	42.15	6.39	33–52
	Dyslexic	36.65	6.64	23–52
	Repeaters	32.50	6.44	25–41

multivariate analysis of variance there were seven measures on which the dyslexics were significantly different, in this analysis of covariance the low- and high-complexity versions of the Oral Cloze Test showed no significant differences. Thus there were five syntactic measures on which the dyslexics were significantly different from the normals (Table 19). Of the three measures on which there were significant regression effects, only one, the Sentence Repetition Test, demonstrated significant differences between the sample groups, after significant regression effects of auditory memory had been taken into account.

Table 15. Test of Significance[a] for the Within-Cells Regression for Auditory Memory for Digits and Auditory Memory for Words on the Syntactic Measures

Roots	F	$df\ hyp$	$df\ err$	p less than
1–2	3.28	18	56	.001[b]
2–2	1.21	8	28	.326

[a] Wilks' lambda criterion was used.
[b] p less than the .001 level of significance.

Table 16. Univariate F Tests of Significance for the Within-Cells Regression on the Syntactic Measures with Two Covariates: Auditory Memory for Digits and Auditory Memory for Words

Measure	$F(1,37)$	MS	p less than
Test of Recognition of Melody Pattern	0.063	0.084	.939
Test of Recognition of Grammaticality	2.601	12.222	.088
NSST	0.548	4.266	.583
Sentence Repetition Test	16.113	76.779	.001[a]
Berry-Talbott Test	1.902	34.385	.164
Grammatic Closure Test	0.585	4.102	.562
Oral Cloze Test, Low Complexity	14.112	37.959	.001[a]
Oral Cloze Test, High Complexity	6.838	12.299	.003[b]
DSS	0.382	3023.965[c]	.685

[a] p less than the .001 level of significance.
[b] p less than the .01 level of significance.
[c] Computed using raw scores.

Table 17. Raw Regression Coefficients for the Syntactic Measures with Two Covariates: Auditory Memory for Digits and Auditory Memory for Words

	Covariate	
Measure	Test of Auditory Memory for Digits	Test of Auditory Memory for Words
Test of Recognition of Melody Pattern	−.03	.00
Test of Recognition of Grammaticality	.30	−.11
NSST	.11	−.08
Sentence Repetition Test	.24	.28
Berry-Talbott Test	.33	.15
Grammatic Closure Test	−.22	−.04
Oral Cloze Test, Low Complexity	.49	.10
Oral Cloze Test, High Complexity	.19	.09
DSS	6.15	−.70

Table 18. Test of Significance[a] between the Sample Groups on the Syntactic Measures with Auditory Memory for Digits and Auditory Memory for Words as the Covariates

F	$df\ hyp$	$df\ err$	p less than
2.82	9	28	.017[b]

[a] Wilks' lambda criterion was used.
[b] p less than the .05 level of significance.

Discussion

We have evidenced an affirmative answer to the primary research question: Are dyslexics with reading comprehension difficulties deficient in syntactic abilities in comparison to normal children? The major hypothesis of this study was confirmed. The clinical observations of Hallgren (1950), Johnson and Myklebust (1965), Orton (1937), Rabinovitch (1959, 1962), and Zangwill (1962) have been given statistical

Table 19. Univariate *F* Tests of Significance between the Sample Groups on the Syntactic Measures with Auditory Memory for Digits and Auditory Memory for Words as the Covariates

Measure	$F(1,37)$	MS	p less than
Test of Recognition of Melody Pattern	15.06	20.13	.001[a]
Test of Recognition of Grammaticality	1.49	6.99	.230
NSST	3.21	24.97	.082
Sentence Repetition Test	4.32	20.60	.045[b]
Berry-Talbott Test	9.02	162.99	.005[c]
Grammatic Closure Test	13.44	94.24	.001[a]
Oral Cloze Test, Low Complexity	1.87	5.04	.180
Oral Cloze Test, High Complexity	2.98	5.36	.093
DSS	6.13	48523.56[d]	.018[b]

[a] p less than the .001 level of significance.
[b] p less than the .05 level of significance.
[c] p less than the .01 level of significance.
[d] Computed from raw scores.

confirmation. The dyslexics were significantly different from normal children in syntactic abilities when the regression effects resulting from auditory memory were partialled out.

The following is a discussion of several questions that were raised by the multivariate analysis of variance and analysis of covariance.

The Sentence Repetition Test Of the three syntactic measures that had significant regression effects related to auditory memory, one measure, the Sentence Repetition Test, is of particular interest. In the analysis of covariance the dyslexics were significantly different from the normal children on the Sentence Repetition Test, even after the significant regression effects had been partialled out. These findings reflect the nature of the task involved in this particular test.

By design semantic difficulty was controlled in the construction of the 20 sentences in this test, thus minimizing the effect of semantic content. The analysis of covariance with receptive vocabulary as the covariate validated the effectiveness of the control, since there were no significant regression effects caused by the semantic variable.

In constructing this test it was obviously impossible to eliminate auditory memory. This factor was controlled, however, in that all of the sentences were either eight or nine words in length. These findings suggest that a sentence repetition test with fewer words per sentence would be a more useful tool to measure syntax in younger children or in children who have limited auditory memory spans. The difficulty lies in the construction of shorter sentences that also vary sufficiently in syntactic complexity to reveal subtle syntactic deficiencies. In any case, it seems impossible to create a sentence repetition test that measures syntactic ability without an interacting auditory memory factor.

Thus the Sentence Repetition Test appears to involve at least two factors: (1) syntactic complexity, which increases gradually and (2) auditory memory, which is approximately the same for each sentence (eight or nine words per sentence).

The high reliability coefficient of .85 for this measure (Table 8) provided an estimate of internal consistency, error, and true variance. Because the number of words per sentence was held constant, the reliability coefficient is mainly a reflection of the syntactic complexity factor.

Our use of the Sentence Repetition Test therefore provides us with an opportunity to examine, first, the importance of auditory memory in sentence repetition and, second, the role of syntactic ability in the repetition of sentences.

The relationships between auditory memory and syntactic ability have been the subject of several investigations, among which are those of Mehler (1963) and Menyuk (1969). The ability to hold in proper sequence a string of words is a prerequisite to our understanding of spoken language. It is thus basic to the integrative process necessary to master the syntax of one's native language (Johnson and Myklebust, 1967).

Although auditory memory plays an important role in the development of receptive language and syntax, there is a reciprocal facilitating role of syntactic ability on auditory memory span for sentences (Miller, 1956). The average auditory memory span for digits or single words in adults is less than the number of words in a sentence that a mature individual can remember. Miller (1967) reported that the number of isolated words that could be recalled by adults was between five and nine but the average number of words in sentence form that could be recalled was 15. He explained this phenomenon in relation to the role of syntax.

Syntax imposes a structure or plan on a series of previously unrelated words, thus allowing the individual to chunk groups of words into grammatical units for the purpose of processing, retention, and recall (Miller, 1967; Fodor and Bever, 1965). Each chunk consists of 2.3–3 words (Miller, 1967). Thus sentence comprehension and recall is a function of both the number of words per sentence and the number of chunks within a sentence.

For the purpose of constructing the Sentence Repetition Test, syntactic complexity was defined as transformational complexity in a developmental sequence (as described in Chapter 2). The number of embedded sentences or chunks increased from two to four, although the number of words per sentence remained the same. Therefore, when that portion of the variance in the Sentence Repetition Test caused by auditory memory span is partialled out, the remaining variance is a reflection of the effect of syntactic complexity on sentence repetition.

In light of these findings and those of Menyuk (1969) and Miller and Ervin (1964), it seems that the ability to chunk words together into grammatical units is a function of syntactic ability. Moreover, this ability seems to be revealed in a sentence repetition test after regression caused by auditory memory span is partialled out. Additional evidence in support of this interpretation is to be found in Miller and Ervin's (1964) study in which omissions in a sentence repetition task were thought to reflect those aspects of grammar not yet mastered. These investigators also found that the sentences that were correctly reproduced in a sentence repetition task resembled the sentences the child generated spontaneously. Menyuk (1969) found that sentences repeated correctly were on a higher level of syntactic competence than those generated in spontaneous language. This observation was explained by Miller and Ervin (1964) as related to the concept of sentence imitation. The function of sentence imitation is to practice the grammatical rules the child has already acquired but not yet mastered (Menyuk, 1969; Miller and Ervin, 1964). A child with limited auditory memory span may not be able to comprehend, chunk, and imitate sentences because they exceed his auditory memory span. Thus he is unable to practice the grammatical rules already acquired or emerging. The importance of imitation, whether it be monologue or self-rehearsing, has been thought to be related to the process of gaining proficiency in and automatizing the grammatical rules (McGrady, 1968; Weir, 1962). Therefore, the link between auditory memory and syntactic ability may be revealed in the task of sentence repetition.

This research suggests the conclusion that there are reciprocal effects of auditory memory and syntactic ability. Therefore, care must be taken to isolate these variables in measurement.

Directions for future research Further investigation of the phenomenon of chunking of syntactic units should involve a comparison of the original sentences in the test with the reproduced sentences of the normal and dyslexic children. One possible way of classifying the errors in the reproduced sentences would be to divide them into the following categories: omissions, repetitions, additions, and substitutions. Also, a comparison could be made of the number of embedded sentences in the original sentence and the number in the reproduced sentence. Finally, because the construction of the 20 sentences represents a developmental sequence according to the DSS Procedure (Lee and Canter, 1971), another comparison could be made: The DSS for the spontaneous language sample could be compared with the DSS for the most difficult sentence each child could repeat correctly. This analysis would provide information concerning Menyuk's (1969) observations that normal children can repeat sentences on a slightly higher level than their spontaneously produced sentences, while children with deviant language cannot.

Such analyses might prove helpful in future interpretations of the information revealed in a sentence repetition test. They might reveal an individual's specific syntactic competencies and weaknesses, and would require much less time than an analysis of a spontaneous language sample.

The Oral Cloze Tests The remaining two measures on which there were significant regression effects caused by auditory memory were the two versions of the Oral Cloze Test (Table 16). When the regression effects were partialled out, there were no significant differences between the two sample groups on these measures (Table 19). These findings present somewhat of a paradox, particularly in light of those from the Sentence Repetition Test.

In the administration of the Oral Cloze Tests, unlike the Sentence Repetition Test, there was no limit on the number of times that the phrases or words before and after the deletion could be repeated (see Appendix F). Despite the possibility of an additional number of presentations, the regression attributable to auditory memory was significant on both the low- and high-complexity versions (Table 16). Some clues as to the importance of auditory memory span and its role in the oral cloze procedure were provided by the children themselves and their test behavior: More requests for repetition of an item were made by the dyslexics than by the normal children; and more two-or-more word responses were made by the dyslexics than by the normal children. In most cases these phrase responses were appropriate to the general context. They also would have been grammatically appropriate had the deletion occurred after the last word read, rather than between the two phrases. This may indicate that some children had difficulty remembering two phrases with a deletion between them, but could retain the final phrase and respond appropriately.

Such responses tend to support the theory that memory influences grammatical performance. But there were other observations that do not seem so readily interpretable as being related to auditory memory: 1. More dyslexics hesitated before responding, and their response latencies were longer than those of the normal children.
2. When children hesitated they were asked whether they would like the sentence reread. On several occasions children responded that they remembered what was read, but just could not think of the word.
3. In such cases children were encouraged to guess, and after having made a guess some expressed dissatisfaction with an incorrect response. Thus there were indications that they had retained the two phrases, could monitor their response, but could not correct it.

There are several possible interpretations in view of these findings and observations. The most obvious is that even though repetition was possible, and the children were encouraged to listen to each item more than twice, the number of words they were required to retain exceeded their auditory memory spans. Repetition, therefore, was ineffectual as a control for the auditory memory factor.

Second, the search-and-find process necessitated by this procedure (simultaneously retaining two phrases separated by a deletion) was a very difficult task for all the subjects. The hesitations on the part of dyslexics were necessary for the search-and-find process. The reason that they required more time to find the correct word may be related to their neurological functioning. A principle from the field of cybernetics is that the efficiency of circuitry is directly related to the number of available circuits. In the case of the dyslexics, the assumed neurological dysfunction may have resulted in fewer available "circuits," thus decreasing the efficiency of the brain. Related to this observation was a more generalized manifestation of decreased efficiency in the neurological functioning of the dyslexics in that the average testing session for the normal children lasted 1.75 hours, while for dyslexics it lasted 2.25 hours. This finding confirmed that of McGrady and Olson (1970), who found a similar decreased efficiency in the functioning of learning disability children.

A third possible interpretation is based on an analysis of those responses that were wild guesses or of those cases when the child could make no guess at all. This interpretation is suggested by the search-and-find aspect of this process. If we assume that the child can remember the two phrases and understands the task, there are at least two possible causes for his failure to respond correctly: (1) He may not know the syntactic construction of the sentence at a conscious level; and (2) he may not be able to retrieve the correct structural word that will be grammatically appropriate. Evidence of retrieval or word-finding difficulty in the dyslexic population has been reported by Johnson and Myklebust (1965, 1967) and Rabinovitch and Ingram (1968); these findings give added support to the latter interpretation.

Fourth, the facilitating role of syntax in sentence repetition was discussed earlier. Weaver (1961) examined the function of the syntactic elements of language through structural-word deletions using the cloze procedure. He concluded that structural words provide the plan for storage and retention. When structural words are deleted, as they were in the two Cloze Tests, many of the words that enhance the listener's auditory memory ability may be removed. It is possible that structural-word deletions are not well suited for the oral cloze procedure because of the nature of the auditory input and because of the role played by syntax and especially structural words in relation to auditory memory.

Directions for future research To determine which of the several possible explanations is most plausible, investigators might find a different scoring technique and further analysis of the data helpful. Instead of the present technique of scoring each response "correct" if it is identical to the deleted word and "incorrect" if it is not, Cromer and Weiner's (1966) technique might be preferable. They scored a response "correct" if it was grammatically appropriate to the text, since if the response was grammatically appropriate, it was assumed that the child had internalized the syntactic structure.

A second alternative method to determine whether retrieval difficulty is the underlying cause for failure would be to administer the same Cloze Test in two ways, first in the usual manner (see Appendix F) and then in a multiple-choice fashion. The danger of overtaxing the auditory memory span must be kept in mind in designing this procedure.

An alternative method to control for the auditory memory factor might prove even more effective than repetition. Control would be built into the test itself if the construction of the sentences and spacing of the deletions were such that the lengths of the phrases before and after the deletions were limited and constant. The effectiveness of such a method can only be demonstrated through future research.

Further research is also needed to explore the usefulness of the Oral Cloze procedure as a measure of syntactic ability. There are three avenues that are in need of further exploration. First, the construction and design of the two versions of the Oral Cloze Test used in this study were of an exploratory nature. Although the two versions did seem to reflect distinct levels of difficulty based on a comparison of mean scores for each version (Table 9), there is no direct evidence of the usefulness of having two versions.

Second, the study provided evidence of the need for improving the reliability of these measures (Table 8). One way this can be accomplished is to increase the number of items. Fifty deletions, which has been the standard number of deletions in written Cloze tests, may be too fatiguing, but certainly ten deletions are too few.

Third, a factor analysis of an Oral Cloze Test, together with syntactic measures and auditory memory tests, in the normal population as compared to a learning disability population with deficits in auditory memory might provide useful information.

Summary

The analysis of covariance confirmed the major hypothesis that dyslexic children are deficient in syntactic abilities in comparison to normal children. It also established that five of the nine measures differentiated between the two sample groups and are potentially useful tools for evaluating syntactic abilities.

FACTOR ANALYSIS OF SYNTAX AND RELATED FUNCTIONS

One further way of analyzing the syntactic measures was through a factor analysis of the nine syntactic measures, the two auditory memory measures, and the receptive vocabulary measure (Program BMDO3M). Factor analysis of the intercorrelation matrix (Table 20) for the 12 variables resulted in six factors. Five of the six eigenvalues

Table 20. Within-Cells Correlation Matrix for Factor Analysis of the Syntactic Measures, the Auditory Measures, and the Receptive Vocabulary Measure.

Variable	Test of Recognition of Melody Pattern	Test of Recognition of Grammaticality	NSST	Sentence Repetition Test	Berry-Talbott Test	Grammatic Closure Test	Oral Cloze Test, Low Complexity	Oral Cloze Test, High Complexity	DSS	PPVT	Test of Memory for Digits
Test of Recognition of Melody Pattern											
Test of Recognition of Grammaticality	.12										
NSST	-.06	-.04									
Sentence Repetition Test	.07	-.06	-.09								
Berry-Talbott Test	.14	.22	.03	.36							
Grammatic Closure Test	.26	.03	.15	.16	.14						
Oral Cloze Test, Low Complexity	.05	.11	-.01	.49	.33	.49					
Oral Cloze Test, High Complexity	.20	.01	-.23	.55	.11	.44	.64				
DSS	.21	.12	-.15	.22	.12	.28	.18	.31			
PPVT	.20	.20	.05	.26	.39	.29	.06	.07	.17		
Test of Memory for Digits	-.06	.19	.03	.36	.23	.15	.59	.38	-.01	-.22	
Test of Memory for Words	.00	-.23	-.15	.67	.27	-.05	.47	.46	-.23	-.01	.30

were greater than 1.00 (Harman, 1960). These six factors and the percentage of communality obtained for each are given in Table 21.

These values and percentages show that Factor I, with an eigenvalue of 3.46, is the single factor which accounts for the largest proportion of the communality, 28.8 per cent. Factors II through V provide eigenvalues similar to each other and vary in percentages of communality from 14.8 to 9.5. When combined with Factor VI, these principle components account for 80.7 per cent of the variance from the 12 measures.

Although it is customary to rotate only those eigenvectors associated with eigenvalues greater than 1.00, in this case the use of six eigenvectors in the rotation provided more identifiable factors. The rotation of the eigenvectors associated with the six eigenvalues according to the Kaiser Varimax criteria (Harman, 1960) revealed the factor patterns and their identifications noted in Table 22.

Variables that had loadings of .5 or greater were grouped under that factor (Harman, 1960). The six factor patterns that emerged are:

Factor I: Auditory Memory
Factor II: Semantics and Morphology
Factor III: Morphology for Expressive Language
Factor IV: Comprehension of Syntax
Factor V: Recognition of Grammaticality
Factor VI: Recognition of Melody Pattern

Their loadings are given in Table 23.

Loadings on the first factor were measures of auditory memory and those syntactic measures in which memory was highly related. The second factor, a semantic one, revealed that morphology for nonsense

Table 21. Eigenvalues and Percentage of Communality over Six Factors

Factor	Eigenvalues	Percentage of Communality over Components	
		Incremental	Cumulative
I	3.46	28.8	28.8
II	1.78	14.8	43.6
III	1.27	10.5	54.2
IV	1.25	10.4	64.6
V	1.14	9.5	74.1
VI	0.79	6.6	80.7

Table 22. Rotated Factor Matrix for the Factor Analysis of the Nine Syntactic Measures, the Two Auditory Memory Measures, and the Receptive Vocabulary Measure

Variable	Factor					
	I	II	III	IV	V	VI
Test of Recognition of Melody Pattern	.02	.11	.11	-.06	.06	.95
Test of Recognition of Grammaticality	-.10	.17	.07	-.08	.88	.08
NSST	-.09	.08	-.08	.88	-.03	-.08
Sentence Repetition Test	.77	.37	.09	-.13	-.13	-.03
Berry-Talbott Test	.38	.66	-.12	.08	.36	.06
Grammatic Closure Test	.20	.09	.72	.43	-.02	.27
Oral Cloze Test, Low Complexity	.78	-.03	.34	.20	.21	.04
Oral Cloze Test, High Complexity	.69	-.08	.48	-.15	-.04	.21
DSS	.06	.16	.74	-.31	.11	-.03
PPVT	-.06	.87	.25	.06	.00	.10
Test of Memory for Digits	.67	-.29	.08	.14	.49	-.13
Test of Memory for Words	.82	.13	-.22	-.19	-.27	.01

Table 23. Loadings of the Six Factor Patterns

Variable	Factor					
	I	II	III	IV	V	VI
Test of Recognition of Melody Pattern						.95
Test of Recognition of Grammaticality					.88	
NSST				.88		
Sentence Repetition Test	.77					
Berry-Talbott Test		.66				
Grammatic Closure Test			.72			
Oral Cloze Test, Low Complexity	.78					
Oral Cloze Test, High Complexity	.69					
DSS			.74			
PPVT		.87				
Test of Memory for Digits	.67					
Test of Memory for Words	.82					
Percentage of Communality	28.8	14.8	10.5	10.4	9.5	6.6

words has much in common with receptive vocabulary. Loadings on the third factor were characterized by morphology in expressive language. The fourth, fifth, and sixth factors each had only one variable that identified them, respectively, as comprehension of syntax, recognition of grammaticality, and recognition of melody pattern.

Factor I: Auditory Memory

Loadings on the first factor were the two measures of auditory memory and three of the nine syntactic measures. These three were the same three for which the analysis of covariance revealed significant regression effects related to the auditory memory factor, namely, Sentence Repetition; Cloze, Low Complexity; and Cloze, High Complexity. This again poses two basic questions discussed earlier: (1) What is the role of auditory memory for syntactic development? (2) What is the relationship between syntax and auditory memory for sentences? The centrality of these questions is reflected in the eigenvalue of 3.46. This factor accounted for approximately 29 per cent of the communality over the components, more than twice that of any other single factor (refer to Table 21).

Factor II: Semantics and Morphology

The second factor reveals that receptive vocabulary has much in common with morphology for nonsense words. In the following discussion of the results of the stepwise discriminant analysis, the lack of significant correlation between the two measures of morphology is reported. The uniqueness of each of these measures is also confirmed by the factor analysis in that the two measures loaded on different factors.

The common denominator that resulted in the loading of the measures of receptive vocabulary and morphology for nonsense words on the same factor is not readily apparent. First, the Receptive Vocabulary Test, the PPVT, involves real words, while the Test for Morphology of Nonsense Words, the Berry-Talbott Test, purposely employs "words" that the children have never heard before. Second, the PPVT is a test of single word meanings in which the syntactic variable is at a minimum, if not eliminated entirely. In contrast, the Berry-Talbott Test requires that the child apply morphological rules to inflect totally unfamiliar words.

One clue as to the similarity between the two measures is that a pictorial stimulus accompanies the auditory stimulus in both, although in each measure the function of the visual stimulus is different. In the PPVT the pictures serve the purpose of presenting multiple-choice answers and allowing for nonverbal, gestural responses. However, in the Berry-Talbott Test the pictures actually depict the auditory input and the desired response.

In both measures it is of critical importance that the subject be able to interpret correctly the visual stimulus. In both measures comprehension of the auditory input is dependent on the visual stimulus. Therefore, in both measures the comprehension aspect has not been limited to the auditory channel. The comprehension of the visual stimulus has also played an important role.

Although the argument has been presented that comprehension of visual stimuli is one possible common denominator that caused these two measures to load on Factor II, the test behavior of the children seemed to minimize the importance of this aspect. The pictures were readily interpreted by most of the subjects, and their major concern was with the auditory stimuli. We would like to suggest that it was mainly the auditory comprehension aspect of both these tests, rather than the visual aspect, that was reflected in the factor analysis. In fact, the Berry-Talbott Language Test was called a test of comprehension of language in its full title (Berry and Talbott, 1966). Also, in discussions of the Receptive Vocabulary Test the word "receptive" has referred to the auditory comprehension aspect of this measure.

Perhaps a prerequisite to inflecting the nonsense words in the Berry-Talbott Test was the child's ability to associate the new "word" with its meaning, i.e., to enlarge his receptive vocabulary.

In language learning receptive vocabulary is acquired by associating the nonverbal experience with its auditory equivalent. In the Berry-Talbott Test the nonverbal experience, the picture, was presented simultaneously with its auditory equivalent, the nonsense word. Learning to associate real words or nonsense words with their full meaning requires that the auditory equivalent be presented in context. For a word to be understood and used its syntactic role or form-class must also be known. Information about a word's syntactic role is acquired through exposure to the word in context, i.e., through comprehension of syntax. Therefore, in the measure of receptive vocabulary comprehension of syntax was also implied, since knowledge of the meaning of a word, even when presented in isolation, implies, to varying degrees, knowledge of the word's syntactic function.

Thus the common denominator in these two tests, as reflected in the factor analysis, was probably the child's ability to comprehend language, which aided him in responding correctly in both the PPVT and the Berry-Talbott Test.

Factor III: Morphology for Expressive Language

The two measures which loaded almost equally (.72 and .74, as reported in Table 23) on this factor were the Grammatic Closure and the DSS. The commonality that resulted in the loading of these two measures on the same factor is not readily apparent. The Grammatic Closure Test is limited by design to the morphological aspects of expressive language while the DSS assesses syntax and morphology in expressive language. The results of the factor analysis suggested the hypothesis that the scoring procedure of the DSS was perhaps heavily weighted in the area of morphology as compared to syntax. In order to test this hypothesis, the points granted for correctly inflected primary and secondary verbs, i.e., morphology, were tallied for each of the 40 subjects and then the grand total of the subscores computed (11,087). Total scores for the sample groups were then tallied (22,964). In this way it was determined that 48 per cent of the grand total on the DSS was attributable to morphological aspects of expressive language thus confirming the hypothesis. This finding combined with the results of the factor analysis seem to indicate that for children of this age both the DDS and Grammatic Closure Test assess the child's ability to apply the rules of morphology to correctly inflect words in expressive language. This factor closely resembles the fifth basic category and is, therefore, identified as morphology for expressive language.

Factor IV: Comprehension of Syntax

Factor IV was readily identifiable because only one measure loaded on it, Comprehension of Syntax (NSST). This factor is the first of three that is identical to one of the basic categories. This indicates the validity of assessing specific areas within the broader concept of syntax. The NSST had a Hoyt reliability coefficient of $r = .59$ (Table 8). This test was considered appropriate for children up to the age of seven years, eleven months (Lee, 1969). Therefore, the low reliability could be a result of the fact that on many items all responses were correct (i.e., the test was too easy for the children in the sample groups, whose mean age was 7.9), thus lowering the reliability. On the other hand, the mean score for the two sample groups was 3 points below the standardization mean for the same age range. Thus the reason for the low reliability is not entirely clear at this time. It would seem, however, that the test is a more reliable instrument for younger children (Hedberg, 1971).

Factor V: Recognition of Grammaticality

One measure loaded on Factor V, recognition of grammaticality. Apparently, the ability to identify correct usage is independent of the ability to comprehend or use syntax in expressive language. Yet self-monitoring one's own language for correct syntax does seem related to the ability to monitor someone else's spoken language. The Recognition of Grammaticality Test also had a low reliability of $r=.49$. The low reliability of this measure and the NSST may be related to the lack of significant differences between the sample groups in the analysis of variance. Two ways to improve the reliability of this measure are the following: (1) An item analysis for level of difficulty could be done and those items that were too easy or too difficult eliminated. The reliability study showed that on some items all children failed; i.e., the level of difficulty of the syntax was above their syntactic ability. Since this test was modeled after all four levels of difficulty, including the high school level, of the Metropolitan Achievement Tests (Durost, 1961), perhaps it would be better to use only the levels appropriate for elementary school-age children as the model. (2) In the construction of this test there was no control for either sentence length or semantic difficulty. Because of the importance of both these variables in oral language measures of syntax, it is possible that the results of the analysis of variance would have been different had these two variables been controlled.

Factor VI: Recognition of Melody Pattern

The sixth factor that was identical to one of the basic categories is recognition of melody pattern. This ability was clearly highly independent, as can be seen from the high loading of .95 of the measure of Recognition of Melody Pattern on Factor VI (Table 23). The low reliability of $r = .51$ may be related to the small number of items in the measure. Nonetheless, the results of the factor analysis seem to indicate that recognition of intonation is an independent ability.

As we have seen, Factors III, IV, V, and VI resemble or are identical to four of the five original categories of syntax: morphology in expressive language, comprehension of syntax, recognition of grammaticality, and recognition of melody pattern, respectively.

Summary and Discussion

Because of the ambiguity concerning the identity of Factors I and II, a factor analysis of these 12 variables with a normal population of sufficient size might prove helpful. Another approach that could be fruitful would be a factor analysis done with only the nine syntactic measures. The auditory memory factor involved in the syntactic measures is possibly masking other information. Similarly, it would be interesting to discover on which factor the Berry-Talbott Test will load when the Receptive Vocabulary Test is excluded.

In summary, six factor patterns emerged in the factor analysis. Loadings on the first factor were measures of auditory memory and those syntactic measures in which memory played an important role. The second factor, a semantic one, revealed that morphology for nonsense words has much in common with receptive vocabulary. Loadings on the third factor were characterized by morphology in expressive language. The fourth, fifth, and sixth factors each had only one variable that identified them as comprehension of syntax, recognition of grammaticality, and recognition of melody pattern, respectively.

These findings lend support to the possibility of devising a theoretical construct of subdivisions within the concept of syntax. They validated four of the original categories or subdivisions suggested in the design of this study. Further research is needed to answer the additional questions that have been raised by these findings.

IDENTIFYING CHILDREN WITH SYNTACTIC DEFICIENCIES

Since nine syntactic measures were used, the question was raised as to which of these nine were the most sensitive and best able to differentiate between the dyslexics with syntactic deficiencies and the normal children. A stepwise discriminant analysis was done and three measures were identified: the Grammatic Closure Test, the Berry-Talbott Test, and the Test of Recognition of Melody Pattern. The Raos V, a stepwise statistic, was used to determine the best discriminators (see Table 24). For the single nonzero eigenvalue of 1.192, the discriminant function, lambda, was $0.393 X_1 + 0.261 X_2 + 0.882 X_3$, where X_1 is the score for the Grammatic Closure Test, X_2 is the score for the Berry-Talbott Test, and X_3 is the score for the Test of Recognition of Melody Pattern. Discriminant scores using the discriminant function were computed for each individual. The discriminant score is that linear composite of the three measures identified as the best discriminators that will maximize group differences. Group membership probabilities for each group centroid based on the discriminant scores are given in Table 25. A histogram showing the distributions of the discriminant scores (converted to scaled scores by the Program EIDISC) for each of the sample groups appears in Figure 3.

Table 24. Raos V Statistic for the Three Best Discriminators among the Syntactic Measures

Variable	Raos V	Chi-Square Value
Grammatic Closure Test	21.05	21.05
Berry-Talbott Test	34.67	13.62
Test of Recognition of Melody Pattern	38.63	3.96

Generally, the results of the stepwise discriminant analysis confirmed the results of the univariate F tests of significance for the syntactic measures in the analysis of covariance. The first and third measures identified by the discriminant analysis (the Grammatic Closure Test and the Test of Recognition of Melody Pattern) were also the two measures that differentiated between the two sample groups at less than the .001 level of significance. The Berry-Talbott Test was the

Table 25. Membership Probabilities for Group Centroids under the Three-Variable Discriminant Function

Group	Probability of Membership in Normal Group	Probability of Membership in Dyslexic Group
Normal	.889	.111
Dyslexic	.011	.989

second of the three measures identified, and it had differentiated between the two sample groups at less than the .005 level of significance.

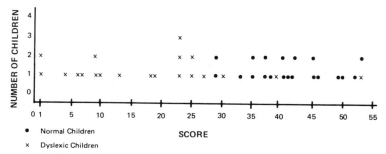

Figure 3. Histogram of the distributions of discriminant scores for the sample groups, based on the three most discriminating syntactic measures. •, Normal children; ×, dyslexic children.

The Test of Recognition of Melody Pattern

Despite the consistency of these results, the reliability coefficient for one measure, the Test of Recognition of Melody Pattern, was low, .49 (Table 8). One way to increase the reliability of this measure would be to increase the number of items, since reliability is a function of the number of items in a test (Guilford, 1954). In its present form it is not useful as a clinical tool for diagnostic purposes, although for research purposes it proved to be a sensitive instrument for differentiating between sample groups. Attempts should be made to develop a clinically useful test of this type.

The Berry-Talbott Language Test of Comprehension of Grammar

This test of morphology for nonsense words had a high reliability coefficient of .89 (Table 8). A comparison of the mean scores of each group for the simple and complex subscores reveals an interesting difference (Table 26).

The means of the simple subscores for the two sample groups were almost identical, while the difference between the means of the complex subscores was slightly more than 5 points. In addition, the simple subscore means represented nearly a perfect score. The complex sub-

Table 26. Means and Ranges for Subscores of the
Berry-Talbott Test

Berry-Talbott Test Subscore	Group	Mean	Range
Simple subscore (Perfect score 10)	Normal	9.75	8–10
	Dyslexic	9.00	6–10
	Repeaters	6.83	2–10
Complex subscore (Perfect score 26)	Normal	16.85	9–21
	Dyslexic	11.50	6–21
	Repeaters	8.67	0–16

score means, in contrast, were between 10 and 15 points less than a perfect score. Apparently, the complex items accounted for most of the difference between the total score means (Table 9) and for the ability of this measure to differentiate between the sample groups. Brittain (1970) also found that first and second graders did equally well on the 19 simple items in Berko's (1958) Test of Morphology, but that the second graders did better than the first graders on the ten complex items.

The Berry-Talbott Test in its present form appears to be a valuable research tool. The novel drawings and words appealed to the children, and most seemed to enjoy this test. In the future it could also become a useful diagnostic tool if normative data were collected. Because of the lack of perfect scores from a sample of 20 college students who were given this test, it is difficult to judge the age range for which this measure is appropriate. Although the manual (Berry and Talbott, 1966) suggests that eight-year-old children are expected to get almost all items correct, this was not found to be the case for the normal group in our study (whose mean age was 7.9). The mean score for this group was 26.60, approximately 9 points less than a perfect score.

The response to the items could also provide valuable clinical information. As an alternative to the scoring method based on the division of items into the two categories, simple and complex, they could be divided into subgroups based on the morphological rules employed by the subject in formulating his response. In this way an individual's profile for internalized, emergent, and unknown morphological rules could be determined, and thus could provide useful information for the clinician or language therapist.

The Grammatic Closure Test

The stepwise discriminant analysis identified the two measures that assessed morphological ability as two of the three best discriminators among the nine syntactic measures. At first glance this appears to be logical, since both measures were tests of morphology. Yet the simple correlation coefficient of the Berry-Talbott Test with the Grammatic Closure Test in the normal group was $r = .20$ and in the dyslexic group, $r = .12$. Apparently the ability to inflect real words correctly, as in the Grammatic Closure Test, is relatively independent of the ability to inflect nonsense words correctly, as in the Berry-Talbott Test. Further indications of the distinct nature of each of these tasks was discussed in the section on factor analysis.

The stepwise discriminant analysis has confirmed the usefulness of the Grammatic Closure Test as a research instrument, despite its low reliability of .68. In addition, the normative data in the manual (Kirk et al., 1968) make this a valuable clinical tool for diagnostic and educational purposes.

Group Membership Probabilities

For the normal and dyslexic groups the group membership probabilities were 89 per cent and 99 per cent, respectively (Table 25). On the basis of these results, we can expect that in the normal population, as described by the selection criteria discussed in Chapter 3, approximately 10 per cent would have some syntactic deficiencies. Moreover, 99 per cent of dyslexic children with reading comprehension difficulties, as described by the selection criteria, can be expected to have syntactic difficulties.

Summary

These findings indicate the importance of assessing syntactic abilities in the evaluation and diagnosis of children with reading comprehension difficulties. They also provide the clinician with information on the syntactic measures that best differentiate between those dyslexics that resemble the normal population in syntactic abilities and those that have deficiencies in syntactic abilities.

SYNTACTIC ABILITY AND READING COMPREHENSION

It was suggested that syntactic ability is related to reading comprehension. A multiple-regression analysis (Program BMD29) was done to explore this relationship in the two sample groups. The criterion used was the reading comprehension score of the Gates-MacGinitie Reading Tests, Primary B. There were a total of 11 measures, which were reduced to three variables. The first, the syntax variable, was comprised of the nine syntactic measures; the second, the decoding variable, was the measure of oral reading of single nonsense words; and the third, the semantic variable, was the measure of receptive vocabulary. The three variables were thought to represent three primary sources of information the reader calls upon to gain meaning from written language: syntactic information, knowledge of grapheme-phoneme correspondences, and semantic information. The purpose of this analysis was to answer the research question: What is the relationship among reading comprehension and the syntactic, semantic, and decoding variables for dyslexic and normal children?

To answer the above research question, we had to determine the proportion of the variance for reading comprehension contributed by each of the three variables (Program BMD29). A multiple correlation coefficient was computed. The criterion was reading comprehension, and the three predictors were the syntax, decoding, and semantic variables. The multiple correlation of reading comprehension with all three variables for the normal group was $r = .86$ and for the dyslexic group, $r = .79$. To determine the proportion of the variance in the criterion attributable to the predictors, we squared the correlation coefficient (R^2). The squared multiple correlations of reading comprehension with each of the three possible pairs of predictors (syntax and decoding, syntax and semantics, and semantics and decoding) and with all three variables are reported for the two sample groups in Table 27. The R^2 values for the pairs and for all three variables (Table 27, columns 1–4) were then used to determine the unique variance for each of the three variables with reading comprehension (Table 28) in the following way: column 4 minus column 3 yields 5, 4 minus 1 yields 6, and 4 minus 2 yields 7. As can be seen, the largest proportion of the unique variance (41 per cent for the dyslexic children and 54 per cent for the normal children) is attributable to the syntax variable. The patterns of unique variance for the two groups are not strikingly

Table 27. R^2 of Reading Comprehension with the Three Predictors

Group	1. Syntax and Decoding	2. Syntax and Semantics	3. Decoding and Semantics	4. All Three
Normal	.62617	.68967	.21242	.74367
Dyslexic	.62256	.57337	.20867	.61952

different, although the overall predictability of reading comprehension was less in the dyslexic group than in the normal group (61 per cent in contrast to 74 per cent).

The unique variance for the two groups for two out of the three predictors, syntax and decoding, are almost identical (Table 28). For the semantic variable there is a considerable discrepancy. In the normal group approximately 12 per cent of the unique variance is attributable to the semantic variable, while for the dyslexic group not even 1 per cent of the unique variance is attributable to this variable. The discrepancy between the two sample groups of 13 per cent in the overall predictability of reading comprehension seems to be related to the lack of unique variance attributed to the semantic variable in the dyslexic group (Table 27).

As was reported, there were no significant differences between the two sample groups in receptive vocabulary. Therefore, it can be assumed that each group possessed an equal amount of semantic information. Thus the discrepancies in overall predictability and in the proportion of unique variance attributed to the semantic variable in the two groups seem to be partially a result of the inability of the dyslexic to use efficiently the semantic information he possesses because of his syntactic deficiencies.

The multiple-regression analysis provided valuable information in support of the theory of reading as a psycholinguistic process (Good-

Table 28. Proportion of the Variance Unique to Each of the Three Predictors

Group	5. Syntax	6. Semantics	7. Decoding
Normal	.53125	.11750	.05400
Dyslexic	.41085	−.00304	.04615

man, 1969a, 1970a; Lerner, 1969, 1971; Ruddell, 1966, 1968). These findings indicate that syntactic information accounts for approximately one-half of the variance in reading comprehension at the second-grade level.

Because of the importance of syntactic ability in reading comprehension, even for the beginning reader, some measure of a child's syntactic competence should be included in the assessment of reading readiness. Similarly, in programs for early identification and prevention of learning difficulties, at the preschool and kindergarten levels, there should be provisions for the identification and education of children with syntactic deficiencies.

The overall predictability of reading comprehension in the normal and dyslexic groups with the three predictors, syntax, semantics and decoding, was 74 and 61 per cent, respectively. Therefore, 16 per cent of the variance in the normal group and 39 per cent in the dyslexic group were unaccounted for by these three predictors. It is possible that had there been more than one measure of decoding ability and of receptive vocabulary, the reliability of these measures as predictors would have been increased and the proportion of the variance unique to each of these two predictors would have been somewhat greater. But because of the small amount of overlap among the three predictors (Tables 27 and 28), it is doubtful that the unique variance attributable to the decoding and semantic variables would have been greatly increased.

In the normal group the variance unique to the semantic variable in predicting reading comprehension was nearly 12 per cent (Table 28). In contrast, in the dyslexic group virtually no contribution was made by the semantic variable. This discrepancy is probably related to the findings of Doehring (1968), and confirmed by this study, regarding differences in the correlations of receptive vocabulary with reading comprehension in the normal and reading disability population. Doehring (1968) reported that reading had a high correlation with oral vocabulary only in the normal population. The simple correlation of reading comprehension with the measure of receptive vocabulary for the normal group in this study was $r = .42$ (significant at the .05 level); in the dyslexic group, $r = -.08$. In view of the fact that there was no significant difference in receptive vocabulary in the analysis of variance between the sample groups, this discrepancy is even more striking. Apparently dyslexic children cannot effectively utilize in the reading process the semantic information they possess. The reason for this is not clear, but a clue may lie in the interrelationship between syntax and semantics.

Words in sentences gain meaning only in relation to other words, namely, within the syntactic structure. It is possible that the dyslexic, because of his syntactic deficiencies, is unable to comprehend the relational aspect of words and therefore is blocked from fully utilizing the semantic information he possesses.

An area of functioning of critical importance in the reading process, but one that was not assessed in this study, is the area of visual processing. Part of the unexplained variance may be the result of visual processing ability. Indirect evidence in support of this possibility comes from studies of visual processing in the dyslexic population.

The occurrence of both visual and auditory processing deficiencies in the dyslexic population has been reported by Doehring (1968), Ingram (1960), Ingram and Reid (1956), and Johnson and Myklebust (1965). If this is the case, then part of the unaccounted-for variance in the normal and dyslexic groups may be attributable to the visual processing deficiencies in the dyslexic group. However, this is only one of many possible explanations of the unaccounted-for variance.

It may also be that assessment of visual processes or other obscure factors is more important for predicting reading comprehension ability in the dyslexic population than in the normal population.

The multiple-regression analysis provided part of the answer to one of the major research questions posed in this study, that of the relationship among reading comprehension and syntactic, semantic, and decoding ability. This question is perhaps the most critical one if the needs of dyslexic children are to be met. Thus these findings have confirmed both the basic assumption of this study, that syntactic ability is important for reading comprehension, and the major hypothesis, that dyslexics have syntactic deficiencies. The focus should now be on the amelioration and prevention of reading comprehension difficulty through identification programs and recommendations for appropriate remediation.

Chapter Five

Summary and Conclusion

Previous research has indicated possible deficiencies in the oral syntax of dyslexic children. The purpose of this investigation was to provide more precise comparisons of the oral syntax of dyslexic children with that of normal children.

On the basis of various theories of language development, syntax was subdivided into the following five categories for measurement: (1) recognition of melody pattern, (2) recognition of grammaticality, (3) comprehension of syntax, (4) sentence repetition, and (5) syntax and morphology in expressive language. Nine specific measures were selected or devised to assess syntactic ability in each category. The nine syntactic measures were chosen in such a way that one measure was used in each of the first four categories and five were used in the fifth category.

A basic assumption in this study was that syntactic ability is related to reading comprehension. The theory of reading as a psycholinguistic process has emphasized the importance of syntactic ability. One of the three kinds of information the reader uses in unlocking words and gaining meaning is syntactic information. A second goal of this study was to determine the relative importance of syntax in reading comprehension in comparison to the importance of knowledge of grapheme-phoneme correspondences and word meanings. For this reason six estimates of reading ability and one of receptive vocabulary were among the measures used.

Because of the importance of auditory memory in syntactic development, two other measures were included. These were measures of auditory memory span for digits and auditory memory span for words. It was thus possible to explore the relationships between syntactic ability and auditory memory.

The major hypothesis of this investigation was that dyslexic children with reading comprehension difficulties are deficient in syntactic abilities in comparison to normal children. The underlying assumption was that syntactic competence is important for reading comprehension.

To test this hypothesis, we selected two sample groups from 11 elementary schools in Evanston, Illinois, School District 65. One group consisted of 20 normal boys, and the other of 20 dyslexic boys. All subjects were monolingual, Caucasian second graders (not repeaters or early entrants), who ranged in age from seven years, four months to eight years, five months. Hearing and visual acuity were within normal limits, and the boys were in good physical and emotional health. For each subject there was evidence of well-developed intelligence and receptive vocabulary, as well as adequate educational and experiential opportunity. Each dyslexic was matched with a normal child who was within three months of his chronological age.

A group of children who met the above criteria were tested initially on two tests of reading comprehension. Each child's classification was based on his performance on these measures. The dyslexics scored 1 SD or more below the mean on these two measures, while the normal children scored at the mean or above. During a period of two months each child was tested individually. The tests assessed four categories of functioning: syntactic ability, receptive vocabulary, auditory memory, and reading. A summary of the results follows.

THE FINDINGS

Syntactic Abilities

The dyslexic children were found to be different from the normal children in syntactic abilities. In three of the five aspects of syntax there were significant differences between the sample groups, in each case favoring the normal children. These three areas were (1) recognition of melody pattern, (2) sentence repetition, and (3) syntax and morphology in expressive language. In two aspects, recognition of grammaticality and comprehension of syntax, there were no significant differences. The low reliability of the two measures in these categories may have contributed to their failure to demonstrate differences between the two groups.

For interpretive purposes a group of six second-grade dyslexic boys who had repeated a grade, but who met every criteria other than age, were tested individually. On eight of the nine syntactic measures the mean score of the repeaters was lower than that of the dyslexic group. Therefore, it seems that neither maturation, exposure to language over a longer period of time, nor continued education was effective in closing the gap between the syntactic ability of the repeaters and that of their younger normal classmates.

To determine the relationship between auditory memory and syntax, we did an analysis of covariance. When the variance attributable to auditory memory was separated out, the difference between the two groups on the syntactic measures was still significant. There was, however, significant regression as a result of the auditory memory factor. After the significant regression effects from the two Oral Cloze Tests, measures of expressive language syntax, had been partialled out, there were nonsignificant differences between the groups. This was not the case for a third measure, the Sentence Repetition Test, on which there were regression effects. After partialling out the regression effects, this measure still differentiated significantly between the groups.

Results of a factor analysis substantiated in part the original subdivision of syntax and the syntactic measures into five categories. Four of the five factors were identified as the following: (1) recognition of melody pattern, (2) recognition of grammaticality, (3) comprehension of syntax, and (4) morphology in expressive language. Each of the first three factors above was identified by one measure which loaded on it. There were two measures that loaded on the fourth factor, morphology in expressive language. These results substantiate to a considerable degree the psychological reality and uniqueness of four of the categories within the broader concept of syntax.

A fifth factor on which three of the syntactic measures loaded was identified as the auditory memory factor in syntactic abilities. These three measures, the two Oral Cloze Tests and the Sentence Repetition Test, were also the three measures for which there was significant regression attributable to the auditory memory factor. The relationship between auditory memory and syntax is evidenced in many areas. Perhaps a clue to unraveling the nature of this relationship can be found by examining the task of sentence repetition, referred to as sentence imitation by Miller and Ervin (1964). The function of sentence imitation is for the child to practice the grammatical rules he has already acquired but not yet mastered (Menyuk, 1969; Miller and Ervin, 1964). A child with limited auditory memory span may not be able to imitate sentences because they exceed his auditory memory span. Therefore, the link between auditory memory and syntactic ability may be revealed in the task of sentence repetition.

Of the five measures that differentiated significantly between the two sample groups after regression caused by auditory memory had been partialled out, three were identified as the best discriminators. These were the Grammatic Closure Test, the Berry-Talbott Test, and the Test of Recognition of Melody Pattern. Because of the low reliability of $r = .49$ of the third measure, it is not considered a useful diagnostic instrument in its present form, but it is a valuable research tool.

There are no normative data available at present for the Berry-Talbott Test. Its high reliability and ability to discriminate between groups makes it an extremely useful measure for research purposes. The Grammatic Closure Test should be a useful measure for screening and diagnostic purposes.

The major hypothesis of the present investigation was confirmed. Dyslexics with reading comprehension difficulties were found to be significantly deficient in oral syntax when compared with normal children.

Reading Comprehension and Syntax

The psycholinguistic theory of reading emphasizes the importance of the reader's oral syntax. A basic assumption of this study was that syntactic ability and the syntax of written material are important sources of information for the reader in the process of reading comprehension.

A multiple-regression analysis provided supportive evidence validating this assumption. The findings indicated that syntactic ability accounted for approximately one-half of the variance in reading comprehension at the second-grade level. In view of the age of the subjects and the fact that the beginning reader's need for visual clues, i.e., attention to grapheme-phoneme correspondences, is greater than that of the mature reader, the findings are remarkable.

The three predictors syntax, semantics, and decoding accounted for approximately three-fourths and two-thirds of the variability in reading comprehension in the normal and dyslexic groups, respectively. It was suggested that this discrepancy in overall predictability between the sample groups may in part be a result of the inability of the dyslexic child to use efficiently the semantic information he possesses because of his syntactic deficiencies.

The variability unaccounted for by these three predictors was perhaps in part attributable to visual processing ability. By design, assessment of visual functioning was not included in this study. Despite this exclusion, it is still surprising that as much as 75 per cent of the variance in normal children could be explained by the three predictors selected, thus confirming the psycholinguistic theory of reading and the importance of syntactic information in reading comprehension.

IMPLICATIONS OF THE FINDINGS

The Normal Population

As in the study of pathology in medicine, where the healthy individual often benefits from the study of the ill, the study of children with learning disabilities has often been beneficial for all children. One of the implications of these findings pertains to the language arts curriculum of the normal child.

We would like to suggest that attention to syntactic growth and development should be part of reading readiness and language arts programs for all children. Language enrichment activities have been the focus of attention in the past decade, especially for the dialectically different child. But the meaning of language enrichment has perhaps been identified too often with vocabulary expansion, rather than with syntactic proficiency. The difficulty lies in the unanswered questions faced by researchers and educators as to how a child acquires syntax and how syntactic development can be enhanced. Bloom (1970), Cazden (1965, 1968a,b, 1969, 1972), McNeill (1970), Moffet (1968a, b), and Smith, Meredith, and Goodman (1970) have been among the major investigators to deal with these questions. Most recently many systematic training programs for small samples of children with deviant language have been developed and employed with promising results (Bricker, 1972; Leonard, 1974; MacDonald and Blott, 1974). As knowledge about the nature of the language learning process and the interaction between cognitive development and linguistic experience accrues, it will be possible to incorporate into the curriculum suggestions for enhancing syntactic development.

Included in the evaluation of reading readiness should be specific measures for assessing syntactic ability. Experimental methods for analyzing child language based on spontaneous speech samples, such as mean length of utterance, weighted scales (as in the DSS), and frequency counts, are presently in use and/or being refined (Cazden, 1971, 1972; Lee and Canter, 1971). An ingenious method for assessing comprehension of specific syntactic structures was devised by Chomsky (1969). Analysis of sentence repetitions has potential as an assessment device (Carrow, 1974; Menyuk, 1969). Three of the nine syntactic measures which comprised the syntactic variable were also identified as valuable screening devices for use with children who are similar to the members of the sample groups.

These findings also have implications for methodology in the teaching of reading. They point to the importance of teaching young children to read not only words in isolation, but also words in phrases and sentences. Furthermore, preprimers and primers written in the syntactic style of the child's spoken language and using syntax that does not exceed his level of development will help the child to become aware of the relationship that exists between spoken and written language and will therefore enhance his reading comprehension. The most important implication for the teaching of reading is that meaning is conveyed primarily through the syntactic structure rather than the individual words. Syntax carries the burden of the message.

The Dyslexic Population

When a child is having difficulty in reading comprehension, there is a high probability that his difficulty is related to syntactic deficiencies. Therefore, the assessment of syntactic ability should be included in the evaluation and diagnostic procedures. A well-standardized measure similar to the Berry-Talbott Language Test of Comprehension of Grammar or the Grammatic Closure Test would be a useful screening device. If the results on the screening measure pointed to a possible deficiency, then further testing in the four areas of syntax identified in this study would be indicated. Recommendations for appropriate remediation could be made on the basis of the test results.

In Chapter 1 the ultimate goal of this study was described as twofold: early identification of dyslexic children with syntactic deficiencies and recommendation for appropriate remediation. The question of early identification is a rather difficult one. Theoretically, a child cannot have difficulty in reading until he is of the age when he is expected to learn to read. But the high incidence of dyslexic children with syntactic deficiencies (approximately 90 per cent) leads us to hypothesize that it would be possible to identify high-risk children prior to first grade on the basis of syntactic abilities. In fact, some innovative programs for identifying and preventing learning difficulties are presently being initiated or are in the blueprint stage. It would seem then that if syntactic measures were incorporated into the evaluation process, potentially dyslexic children could be identified and, with appropriate intervention, their reading comprehension difficulties minimized.

IMPLICATIONS FOR FURTHER RESEARCH

Further Analysis of the Data

It was suggested that three tests, the Sentence Repetition Test and the two Oral Cloze Tests, be rescored and analyzed. In the Sentence Repetition Test the classification of errors as repetitions, additions, substitutions, or omissions would provide useful information. Also, an overall score for each child could be a ratio of the total number of embedded sentences in his repetitions to the total number of embedded sentences in the original sentences read by the examiner.

In the Oral Cloze Tests each response would be scored "correct" if it were grammatically appropriate within the sentence. In this way a child with word-finding problems would not be penalized. The mean number of grammatically appropriate responses of the dyslexics would then be compared with the mean of the normal children. This scoring method may be a more sensitive technique for assessing syntactic ability.

The factor analysis procedure was revealing and perhaps could be useful in further delineating the categories within syntactic ability if the nine syntactic measures were analyzed first by themselves (nine measures), then together with the semantic variable (ten measures), and finally with the two auditory memory measures (11 measures).

By increasing the size of the normal and dyslexic groups to approximately four times the number of variables factored (48 in each group), the four possible combinations of the 12 measures (9, 10, 11, and 12) could be factored with the normal and dyslexic groups individually.

The Syntactic Measures Used

Several measures were experimental, and therefore no normative data were available. Suggestions for further refinement of these measures are as follows: (1) standardization of the Berry-Talbott Test, (2) extension of the norms for the DSS to include older children, (3) revision and standardization of the Test of Recognition of Grammaticality, (4) increasing the number of items in and standardization of the Test of Recognition of Melody Pattern, (5) an item analysis and standardization of the Sentence Repetition Test, and (6) revision and standardization of the Oral Cloze Tests for control of phrase lengths before and after deletions.

CONCLUSIONS

The present study suggests that most dyslexic children with reading comprehension difficulties are deficient in syntactic abilities in comparison to normal children. It is felt that this finding generalizes beyond the 20 boys who comprised the dyslexic group. It has implications regarding the nature of dyslexia, its diagnosis, and its remediation.

This study has delineated what previously may have been referred to as "accompanying language deficits" or as primitive or immature syntax in dyslexia (Hallgren, 1950; Johnson and Myklebust, 1965; Orton, 1937; Rabinovitch, 1959, 1962; Rabinovitch and Ingram, 1968; Zangwill, 1962). It seems that further research to refine and standardize the measures used in this investigation is warranted. The dyslexic child, because of his syntactic deficiencies, may be more handicapped than was previously thought. Recognizing this difficulty is the first and most critical step toward appropriate intervention. Thus it seems that dyslexia is a specific reading disability accompanied in most cases by syntactic deficiencies that contribute to reading comprehension difficulties.

References

Abrams, J. 1968. "Dyslexia—Single or plural?" Paper presented at N.R. Conference (December, 1968).

Anderson, I. H., W. F. Dearborn, and G. Fairbanks. 1937. "Common and Differential Factors in Reading Vocabulary and Hearing Vocabulary." *Journal of Educational Research* 30: 317—324.

Bailey, B. 1968. "Some Aspects of the Impact of Linguistics on Language Teaching in Disadvantaged Communities." *Elementary English* 45(5): 570—578.

Baker, H. J., and B. Leland. 1959. *Detroit Tests of Learning Aptitude.* Indianapolis: Bobbs-Merrill.

Bar-Hillel, Y. 1964. *Language and Information: Selected Essays on Their Theory and Application.* Reading, Mass., and Jerusalem: Addison-Wesley and Jerusalem Academic Press.

Barton, A. 1963. "Reading Research and Its Communication: The Columbia-Carnegie Project." *In* A. Figurel (ed.), *Reading as an Intellectual Activity.* International Reading Association Conference Proceedings, Vol. 8. Newark, Del.: International Reading Association.

Bateman, B. 1965. "An Educator's View of a Diagnostic Approach to Learning Disorders." *Learning Disorders, I.* Seattle: Seattle Seguin School.

Beaver, J. 1968. "Transformational Grammar and the Teaching of Reading." *Research in the Teaching of English* 2(3): 161—171.

Bender, L. 1958. *Problems in Conceptualization and Communication in Children with Developmental Alexia Psychopathology and Communications.* New York: Grune and Stratton.

Bereiter, C., and S. Engelmann. 1966. *Teaching Disadvantaged Children in the Preschool.* Englewood Cliffs, N.J.: Prentice-Hall.

Berko, J. 1958. "The Child's Learning of English Morphology." *Word* 14: 150—177.

Berko, J. 1961. "The Child's Learning of English Morphology." *In* S. Saporta (ed.), *Psycholinguistics: A Book of Readings.* New York: Holt, Rinehart and Winston.

Bernstein, B. 1961. "Social Structure, Language and Learning." *Educational Research* 3: 163—176.

Bernstein, B. 1964. "Elaborated and Restricted Codes: Their Social Origin and Some Consequences." *American Anthropologist* P. 2, 66: 55—69.

Berry, M., and Talbott. 1966. *Berry-Talbott Language Tests, 1. Comprehension of Grammar.* Rockford, Ill.

Berry, M. 1969. *Language Disorders of Children.* New York: Appleton-Century-Crofts.

Betts, E. A. 1954. "Unsolved Problems of Reading." *Elementary English* 31: 325—329.

Bloom, L. 1968. "Language Development: Form and Function in Emerging Grammars. Ph.D. dissertation, Columbia University.

Bloom, L. 1970. *Language Development: Form and Function in Emerging Grammars.* Cambridge, Mass.: The M.I.T. Press.

Bormuth, J. 1968a. "New Measures of Grammatical Complexity." *In* K. Goodman (ed.), *The Psycholinguistic Nature of the Reading Process.* Detroit: Wayne State University Press.

Bormuth, J. 1968b. *Readability in 1968—A Research Bulletin.* National Council of Teachers of English. Chicago: The University of Chicago Press.

Bormuth, J. 1969. *Development of Readability Analyses.* U.S. Department of Health, Education and Welfare, Office of Education, Bureau of Research, Project No. 7-0052, Contract No. OEC-3-7-070052-0326.

Bougere, M. 1969. "Selected Factors in Oral Language Related to First-Grade Reading Achievement." *Reading Research Quarterly* 5(1): 31–58.

Bricker, W. A. 1972. "A Systematic Approach to Language Training." *In* R. L. Schiefelbusch (ed.), *Language of the Mentally Retarded.* Baltimore: University Park Press.

Brinton, J. E., and W. A. Danielson. 1958. "A Factor Analysis of Language Elements Affecting Readability." *Journalism Quarterly* 35: 420–426.

Brittain, M. 1970. "Inflectional Performance and Early Reading." *Reading Research Quarterly* 6(1): 34–48.

Brown, R., and U. Bellugi. 1964. "Three Processes in the Child's Acquisition of Syntax." *In* E. Lenneberg (ed.), *New Direction in the Study of Language.* Cambridge, Mass.: The M.I.T. Press.

Brown, R., and C. Fraser. 1964. "The Acquisition of Syntax." *Child Development Monographs* 29: 43–79.

Brown, R., and C. Fraser. 1968. "The Development of wh-Questions in Child Speech." *Journal of Verbal Learning and Verbal Behavior* 7: 279–290.

Caldwell, B. 1967. *The Preschool Inventory.* Princeton, N.J.: Educational Testing Service.

Carrow, E. 1968. *Auditory Comprehension Test of Language Structure.*

Carrow, E. 1974. "A Test Using Elicited Imitations in Assessing Grammatical Structure in Children." *Journal of Speech and Hearing Disorders* 39(4): 437–444.

Cazden, C. 1965. "Environmental Assistance to the Child's Acquisition of Grammar." Ph.D. dissertation, Harvard University.

Cazden, C. 1968a. "The Acquisition of Noun and Verb Inflections." *Child Development* 39: 433–448.

Cazden, C. 1968b. "Some Implications of Research on Language Development for Preschool Education." *In* R. D. Hess and R. M. Bears (eds.), *Early Education.* Chicago: Aldine.

Cazden, C. 1969. "Suggestions from Studies of Language Acquisition." *Childhood Education* 46: 127–131.

Cazden, C. 1971. "Evaluating Language and Learning in Early Childhood Education." *In* B. S. Bloom, T. Hastings, and C. Madaus (eds.),

Handbook for Formative and Summative Evaluation of Student Learning. New York: McGraw-Hill.

Cazden, C. 1972. *Child Language and Education.* New York: Holt, Rinehart and Winston.

Chall, J. 1967. *The Great Debate.* New York: McGraw-Hill.

Chomsky, C. 1969. *The Acquisition of Syntax in Children from 5 to 10.* Cambridge, Mass.: The M.I.T. Press.

Chomsky, N. 1957. *Syntactic Structures.* (Janua Linguarum, Series Minor 4.) The Hague: Mouton.

Chomsky, N. 1965. *Aspects of the Theory of Syntax.* Cambridge, Mass.: The M.I.T. Press.

Clay, M. 1968. "A Syntactic Analysis of Reading Errors." *Journal of Verbal Learning and Verbal Behavior* 7: 634–638.

Coleman, E. B. 1962. "Improving Comprehensibility by Shortening Sentences." *Journal of Applied Psychology* 46: 131–134.

Coleman, E. B. 1964. "The Comprehensibility of Several Grammatical Transformations." *Journal of Applied Psychology* 48: 186–190.

Coleman, E. B. 1965. "Responses to a Scale of Grammaticalness." *Journal of Verbal Learning and Verbal Behavior* 4: 521–527.

Cooperative Primary Tests. 1967. Princeton, N.J.: Educational Testing Service.

Critchley, M. 1964. *Developmental Dyslexia.* London: William Heinemann Medical Books.

Cromer, W., and M. Weiner. 1966. "Idiosyncratic Response Patterns among Good and Poor Readers." *Journal of Consulting Psychology* 30(1): 1–10.

de Hirsch, K. 1968. "Specific Dyslexia or Strephosymbolia." *In* G. Natchez (ed.), *Children with Reading Problems.* New York: Basic Books.

de Hirsch, K., J. F. Jansky, and W. Langford. 1966. *Predicting Reading Failure.* New York: Harper and Row.

Deutsch, M. 1965. "The Role of Social Class in Language Development and Cognition." *American Journal of Orthopsychiatry* 35: 78–88.

Doehring, D. G. 1968. *Patterns of Impairment in Specific Reading Disability.* Bloomington, Ind.: Indiana University Press.

Dunn, L. 1965. *Peabody Picture Vocabulary Test.* Circle Pines, Minn.: American Guidance Service.

Durost, W. N. (ed.). 1961. *Metropolitan Achievement Tests.* New York: Harcourt, Brace and World.

Eisenberg, L. 1966. "The Epidemiology of Reading Retardation and a Program for Preventive Intervention." *In* J. Money (ed.), *The Disabled Reader—Education of the Dyslexic Child.* Baltimore: The Johns Hopkins Press.

Emig, J. 1965. "Grammar and Reading." *In* H. A. Robinson (ed.), *Recent Developments in Reading,* Vol. 26. Proceedings of the Annual Conference on Reading Held at the University of Chicago, 1965. Chicago: The University of Chicago Press.

Ervin, S. 1964. "Imitation and Structural Change in Children's Language." *In* E. Lenneberg (ed.), *New Direction in the Study of Language.* Cambridge, Mass.: The M.I.T. Press.

Ervin, S., and W. Miller. 1963. "Language Development." *In* H. W. Stevenson, T. Kagan, and C. Spiker (eds.), *Child Psychology. Yearbook of the National Society for the Study of Education* 62 (Part I): 108—143.

Flesch, R. 1948. "A New Readability Yardstick." *Journal of Applied Psychology* 32: 221—233.

Fodor, J., and T. Bever. 1965. "The Psychological Reality of Linguistic Segments." *Journal of Verbal Learning and Verbal Behavior* 4: 414—420.

Fraser, C., U. Bellugi, and R. Brown. 1963. "Control of Grammar in Imitation, Comprehension and Production." *Journal of Verbal Learning and Verbal Behavior* 2: 121—135.

Fries, C. 1952. *The Structure of English.* New York: Harcourt Brace.

Gates, A., and W. MacGinitie. 1965. *Gates-MacGinitie Reading Tests.* New York: Teachers College Press, Columbia University.

Gates, A., and A. McKillop. 1962. *Gates-McKillop Reading Diagnostic Tests.* New York: Teachers College Press, Columbia University.

Gleason, J. B. 1969. "Language Development in Early Childhood." *In* J. Walden (ed.), *Oral Language and Reading.* Champaign, Ill.: National Council of Teachers of English.

Goodman, K. 1969a. "An Analysis of Oral Reading Miscues: Applied Psycholinguistics." *Reading Research Quarterly* 5(1): 9—30.

Goodman, K. 1969b. "Dialect Barriers to Reading Comprehension." *In* A. Binter, J. Dlabal, and L. Kise (eds.), *Readings on Reading.* Scranton, Pa.: International Textbook Co.

Goodman, K. 1970a. "Dialect Rejection and Reading: A Response." *Reading Research Quarterly* 5(4): 600—603.

Goodman, K. 1970b. "Reading: A Psycholinguistic Guessing Game." *In* H. Singer and R. Ruddell (eds.), *Theoretical Models and Processes of Reading.* Newark, Del.: International Reading Association.

Guilford, J. P. 1954. *Psychometric Methods.* New York: McGraw-Hill.

Hallgren, B. 1950. "Specific Dyslexia (Congenital Word Blindness): Clinical and Genetic Study." *Acta Psychiatric Neurology,* Suppl. 65: 1—287.

Harlow, H. 1949. "The Formation of Learning Sets." *Psychological Review* 56: 51—65.

Harman, H. 1960. *Modern Factor Analysis.* Chicago: The University of Chicago Press.

Harris, A. 1968. "Diagnosis and Remedial Instruction." *In* H. Robinson (ed.), *Innovation and Change in Reading Instruction.* 67th Yearbook of the National Society for the Study of Education, Part II. Chicago: The University of Chicago Press.

Harris, A. 1970. *How to Increase Reading Ability,* 5th ed. New York: David McKay.

Hedberg, N. 1971. "Environmental Influences on Language Development." Ph.D. dissertation, Northwestern University.

Hepburn, A. 1968. "The Performance of Normal Children of Differing Reading Ability on the ITPA." Ph.D. dissertation, University of Minnesota.

Hermann, K. 1959. *Reading Disability.* Springfield, Ill.: Charles C Thomas.

Hildreth, G. 1935. "An Individual Study in Word Recognition." *Elementary School Journal* 35: 606–619.

Hildreth, G. 1964. "Linguistic Factors in Early Reading Instruction." *Reading Teacher* December: 173–178.

Hill, R. 1961. "Grammaticality." *Word* 17: 1–10.

Hinshelwood, J. 1917. *Congenital Word Blindness.* London: Lewis.

Holmes, J. 1954. "Factors Underlying Major Reading Disabilities at the College Level." *Genetic Psychology Monographs* 49: 3–95.

Hoyt, C. 1941. "Test of Reliability Estimated by Analysis of Variance." *Psychometrika* 6: 153–160.

Hunt, J. 1961. *Intelligence and Experience.* New York: The Ronald Press.

Hunt, K., W. Loban, and R. Strickland. 1970. "Response to 'How Not to Analyze the Syntax of Children,' by Roger McCaig." *Elementary English* 48(5): 619–623.

Hyatt, G. 1968. *Some Psycholinguistic Characteristics of First Graders Who Have Reading Problems at the End of Second Grade.* Ph.D. dissertation, University of Oregon.

Ingram, T. T. S. 1960. "Pediatric Aspects of Specific Developmental Dysphasia, Dyslexia, and Dysgraphia." *Cerebral Palsy Bulletin* 2: 254–267.

Ingram, T. T. S., and J. F. Reid. 1956. "Developmental Aphasia Observed in a Department of Child Psychiatry." *Archives of Diseases of Childhood* 31: 131–161.

Jacobs, R., and P. Rosenbaum. 1968. *English Transformational Grammar.* Waltham, Mass.: Blaisdell.

Jastak, J., and S. Jastak. 1965. *The Wide Range Achievement Test.* Wilmington: Guidance Associates.

Johnson, D., and H. Myklebust. 1965. "Dyslexia in Childhood." *In* J. Hellmuth (ed.), *Learning Disability,* Vol. 1. Seattle: Special Child Publications.

Johnson, D., and H. Myklebust. 1967. *Learning Disabilities: Educational Principles and Practices.* New York: Grune and Stratton.

Jones, L., and J. Wepman. 1961. *Studies in Aphasia: An Approach to Testing.* Chicago: The University of Chicago Industrial Relations Center.

Kass, C. 1966. "Psycholinguistic Disabilities of Children with Reading Problems." *Exceptional Children* 32: 533–539.

Kinsbourne, M., and E. K. Warrington. 1966. "Developmental Factors in Reading and Writing Backwardness." *In* J. Money (ed.), *The Disabled Reader.* Baltimore: The Johns Hopkins Press.

Kirk, S., J. McCarthy, and W. Kirk. 1968. *The Illinois Test of Psycholinguistic Abilities,* rev. ed. Urbana: University of Illinois Press.

Klima, E., and U. Bellugi. 1966. "Syntactic Regularities in the Speech of Children." *In* J. Lyons and R. Wales (eds.), *Psycholinguistics Papers.* Edinburgh: Edinburgh University Press.

Lee, L. 1969. *The Northwestern Syntax Screening Test.* Evanston, Ill.: Northwestern University Press.

Lee, L. 1970. "A Screening Test for Syntax Development." *Journal of Speech and Hearing Disorders* 35(2): 103–112.

Lee, L., and S. Canter. 1971. "Developmental Sentence Scoring: A Clinical Procedure for Estimating Syntactic Development in Children's Spontaneous Speech." *Journal of Speech and Hearing Disorders* 36: 315–340.

Lefevre, C. 1964. *Linguistics and the Teaching of Reading.* New York: McGraw-Hill.

Lenneberg, E. (ed.). 1964. *New Directions in the Study of Language.* Cambridge, Mass.: The M.I.T. Press.

Leonard, L. B. 1974. "A Preliminary View of Generalization in Language Training." *Journal of Speech and Hearing Disorders* 39(4): 429–436.

Lerea, L. 1958. "Assessing Language Development." *Journal of Speech and Hearing Research* 1: 75–85.

Lerner, J. 1969. "A Global Theory of Reading and Linguistics." *In* A. Binter, J. Dlabal, and L. Kise (eds.), *Readings on Reading.* Scranton, Pa.: International Textbook Co.

Lerner, J. 1971. *Children with Learning Disabilities: Theories, Diagnosis and Teaching Strategies.* Boston: Houghton Mifflin.

Loban, W. 1969. "Oral Language and Learning." *In* J. Walden (ed.), *Oral Language and Reading.* Champaign, Ill.: National Council of Teachers of English.

McCarthy, D. 1946. "Language Development in Children." *In* L. Carmichael (ed.), *Manual of Child Psychology.* New York: Wiley.

MacDonald, J. D., and J. P. Blott. 1974. "Environmental Language Intervention: The Rationale for a Diagnostic and Training Strategy through Rules, Context, and Generalization." *Journal of Speech and Hearing Disorders* 39(3): 244–256.

McGrady, H. 1964. "Verbal and Non Verbal Functions in School Children with Speech and Language Disorders." Ph.D. dissertation, Northwestern University.

McGrady, H. 1968. "Language Pathology and Learning Disabilities." *In* H. Myklebust (ed.), *Progress in Learning Disabilities.* New York: Grune and Stratton.

McGrady, H., and D. Olson. 1970. "Visual and Auditory Learning Processes in Normal Children and Children with Specific Learning Disabilities." *Exceptional Children* 36: 581–588.

McNeill, D. 1966. "Developmental Linguistics." *In* F. Smith and G. A. Miller (eds.), *The Genesis of Language: A Psycholinguistic Approach.* Cambridge, Mass.: The M.I.T. Press.

McNeill, D. 1970. *The Acquisition of Language.* New York: Harper and Row.

Mehler, J. 1963. "Some Effects of Grammatical Transformation on the Recall of English Sentences." *Journal of Verbal Learning and Verbal Behavior* 2: 346–351.

Menyuk, R. 1969. *Sentences Children Use.* Cambridge, Mass.: The M.I.T. Press.

Menzel, P. 1970. "The Linguistic Bases of the Language of Writing Items for Instruction Stated in Natural Language." *In* J. Bormuth (ed.), *On the Theory of Achievement Test Items.* Chicago: The University of Chicago Press.

Miller, G. 1956. "The Magical Number Seven, Plus or Minus Two." *Psychological Review* 63: 81–97.

Miller, G. 1962. "Some Psychological Studies in Grammar." *American Psychologist* 17: 748–762.

Miller, G. 1967. *The Psychology of Communication.* New York: Basic Books.

Miller, G., and N. Chomsky. 1963. "Finitary Models of Language Users." *In* R. D. Luce, R. Bush, and E. Galanter (eds.), *Handbook of Mathematical Psychology.* New York: Wiley.

Miller, G., and S. Ervin. 1964. "Imitation and Structural Change in Children's Language." *In* E. Lenneberg (ed.), *New Directions in the Study of Language.* Cambridge, Mass.: The M.I.T. Press.

Moffet, J. 1968a. *An Integrated Curriculum in Language Arts, K-12.* Boston: Houghton Mifflin.

Moffet, J. 1968b. *Teaching the Universe of Discourse.* Boston: Houghton Mifflin.

Monroe, M., and B. Rogers. 1964. *Foundations for Reading.* Chicago: Scott, Foresman.

Myklebust, H. 1954. *Auditory Disorders in Children.* New York: Grune and Stratton.

Myklebust, H. 1964. *The Psychology of Deafness: Sensory Deprivation, Learning and Adjustment,* 2nd ed. New York: Grune and Stratton.

Myklebust, H. 1965. *Development and Disorders of Written Language. Vol. 1: Picture Story Language Test.* New York: Grune and Stratton.

Myklebust, H. 1967. "Psychoneurological Learning Disorders in Children." *In* E. Frierson and W. Barbe (eds.), *Educating Children with Learning Disabilities: Selected Readings.* New York: Appleton-Century-Crofts.

Myklebust, H., and B. Boshes. 1960. "Psychoneurological Learning Disorders in Children." *Archivos de Pediatria* 77: 247–256.

Myklebust, H., and B. Boshes. 1969. *Minimal Brain Damage in Children: Final Report.* (U.S. Public Health Service Contract 108-65-142, Department of Health, Education and Welfare.) Evanston, Ill.: Northwestern University Press.

Orton, A. T. 1937. *Reading, Writing and Speech Problems in Children.* New York: W. W. Norton.

Orton, M. 1957. "The Orton Story." *Bulletin of the Orton Society* 7.

Otis, A., and Lennon, R. 1967. *Otis-Lennon Mental Ability Test.* New York: Harcourt, Brace and World.

Rabinovitch, R. D. 1959. "Reading and Learning Disabilities." *In* S. Arieti (ed.), *American Handbook of Psychiatry.* New York: Basic Books.

Rabinovitch, R. D. 1962. "Dyslexia: Psychiatric Considerations." *In* J. Money (ed.), *Reading Disability Progress and Research Needs in Dyslexia.* Baltimore: The Johns Hopkins Press.

Rabinovitch, R. D., and W. Ingram. 1968. "Neuropsychiatric Considerations in Reading Retardation." *In* G. Natchez (ed.), *Children with Reading Problems.* New York: Basic Books.

Rankin, E. 1957. "An Evaluation of the Cloze Procedure as a Technique for Measuring Reading Comprehension." Ph.D. dissertation, The University of Michigan.

Rankin, E. 1959. "The Cloze Procedure—Its Validity and Utility." *In* O. S. Causey and W. Eller (eds.), *Eighth Yearbook of the National Reading Conference* 8: 131–144.

Rankin, E. 1965. "The Cloze Procedure—A Survey of Research." *In* E. Thurston and L. Hofner (eds.), *The Philosophical and Sociological Bases of Reading.* 14th Yearbook of the National Reading Conference. Milwaukee: National Reading Conference.

Reed, D. 1969. "Linguistics and Reading Once More." *In* J. Walden (ed.), *Oral Language and Reading.* Champaign, Ill.: National Council of Teachers of English.

Robinson, H. 1949. *Clinical Studies in Reading.* Chicago: The University of Chicago Press.

Rubenstein, E. 1968. *The Nominal Sentence* (in contemporary Hebrew). Israel: Hakibbutz Hameuchad.

Ruddell, R. 1965*a*. "The Effect of Oral and Written Patterns of Language Structure on Reading Comprehension." *The Reading Teacher* 18: 270–275.

Ruddell, R. 1965*b*. "Reading Comprehension and Structural Redundancy in Written Material." *In* A. Figurel (ed.), *Reading and Inquiry. IRA Conference Proceedings,* Vol. 10.

Ruddell, R. 1966. "Reading Instruction in First Grade with Varying Emphasis on the Regularity of Grapheme-Phoneme Correspondences and the Relationship of Language Structure to Meaning." *The Reading Teacher* 19: 653–660.

Ruddell, R. 1968. "The Relation of Regularity of Grapheme-Phoneme Correspondences and of Language Structure to Achievement in First-Grade Reading." *In* K. Goodman (ed.), *The Psycholinguistic Nature of the Reading Process.* Detroit: Wayne State University Press.

Ryan, E., and M. Semmel. 1969. "Reading as a Constructive Language Process." *Reading Research Quarterly* 5: 59–83.

Rystrom, R. 1970*a*. "Toward Defining Comprehension: A First Report." *Journal of Reading Behavior* 2: 56–73.

Rystrom, R. 1970*b*. "Toward Defining Comprehension: A Second Report." *Journal of Reading Behavior* 2: 144–157.

Schlesinger, I. 1968. *Sentence Structure and the Reading Process.* The Hague: Mouton.

Schonell, F. 1952. *The Psychology and Teaching of Reading.* London: Oliver and Boyd.

Schuell, H., J. Jenkins, and E. Jimenez-Parson. 1964. *Aphasia in Adults: Diagnosis, Prognosis and Treatment.* New York: Harper and Row, Hoeber Medical Division.

Shuy, R. 1968. "Some Language and Cultural Differences in a Theory of Reading." *In* K. Goodman and J. Fleming (eds.), *Psycholinguistics and the Teaching of Reading.* Newark, Del.: International Reading Association.

Slobin, D. I. 1966. "Grammatical Transformations and Sentence Comprehension in Childhood and Adulthood." *Journal of Verbal Learning and Verbal Behavior* 5: 219–227.

Slobin, D. I., and C. Welsh. 1967. "Elicited Imitation as a Research Tool in Developmental Psycholinguistics." Unpublished manuscript. Department of Psychology, University of California at Berkeley.

Smith, E., R. Meredith, and K. Goodman. 1970. *Language and Thinking in The Elementary School.* New York: Holt, Rinehart and Winston.

Smith, M. 1969. "Reading for the Culturally Disadvantaged." *In* A. Binter, J. Dlabal, and L. Kise (eds.), *Readings on Reading.* Scranton, Pa.: International Textbook Co.

Stevens, M. 1965. "Intonation in the Teaching of Reading." *Elementary English* 42: 231–237.

Stolurow, L. M., and J. R. Newman. 1959. "A Factorial Analysis of Objective Features Presumably Related to Reading Difficulty." *Journal of Educational Research* 52: 243–251.

Strickland, R. 1962. "The Language of Elementary School Children: Its Relationship to the Language of Reading Textbooks and the Quality of Reading of Selected Children." *Bulletin of the School of Education* 38: 1–129.

Stroud, J., A. Hieronymous, and P. McKee. 1957. *Primary Reading Profiles.* Boston: Houghton Mifflin.

Tatham, S. 1970. "Reading Comprehension of Materials Written with Select Oral Language Patterns: A Study at Grades Two and Four." *Reading Research Quarterly* 5(3): 402–426.

Taylor, W. 1953. "A New Tool for Measuring Reliability." *Journalism Quarterly* 30: 415–433.

Taylor, W. 1956. "Recent Developments in the Use of the 'Cloze Procedure.' " *Journalism Quarterly* 33: 42–48.

Templin, M. 1957. *Certain Language Skills in Children: Their Development and Interrelationships.* Minneapolis: University of Minnesota Press.

Terman, L., and M. Merrill. 1960. *Stanford-Binet Intelligence Scale.* Cambridge, Mass.: Houghton Mifflin.

Thorndike, E. 1931. *A Teacher's Word Book of the Twenty Thousand Words.* New York: Teachers College Press, Columbia University.

United States Office of Health, Education and Welfare. 1969. *Reading Disorders in the United States.* Report of the Secretary's National

Advisory Committee on Dyslexia and Related Reading Disorders. Washington, D.C.: U.S. Government Printing Office.

Van Roekel, B. 1968. *H & R Second Year Readiness Test.* New York: Harper and Row.

Venezky, R., and R. Calfee. 1970. "The Reading Competency Model." *In* H. Singer and R. Ruddell (eds.), *Theoretical Models and Processes of Reading.* Newark, Del.: International Reading Association.

Vernon, M. D. 1958. *Backwardness in Reading: A Study of Its Nature and Origin.* Cambridge: Cambridge University Press.

Vogel, S. A. "Morphological Ability in Normal and Dyslexic Children." *Journal of Learning Disabilities.* In press.

Wardhaugh, R. 1969. *Reading: A Linguistic Perspective.* New York: Harcourt, Brace and World.

Weaver, W. 1961. "An Examination of Some Differences in Oral and Written Language Using the Cloze Procedure." Ph.D. dissertation, University of Georgia.

Weber, R.-M. 1968. "The Study of Oral Reading Errors—A Survey of the Literature." *Reading Research Quarterly* 4(1): 96–119.

Weber, R.-M. 1970. "A Linguistic Analysis of First-Grade Reading Errors." *Reading Research Quarterly* 5(1): 427–451.

Wechsler, D. 1949. *Wechsler Intelligence Scale for Children.* New York: The Psychological Corporation.

Weiner, M., and W. Cromer. 1967. "Reading and Reading Difficulty: A Conceptual Analysis." *Harvard Educational Review* 4(37): 620–643.

Weir, R. 1962. *Language in the Crib.* The Hague: Mouton.

Wepman, J. 1951. *Recovery from Aphasia.* New York: The Ronald Press.

Whipple, G., and M. Black. 1966. *Reading for Children Without—Our Disadvantaged Youth.* Newark, Del.: International Reading Association.

Winer, B. 1962. *Statistical Principles in Experimental Design.* New York: McGraw-Hill.

Wolski, W. 1962. *The Michigan Picture Language Inventory.* Ann Arbor: The University of Michigan.

Yngve, V. H. 1968. "A Model and Hypothesis for Language Structure." *In* G. W. Corner (ed.), *Proceedings of the American Philosophical Society,* p. 104. Philadelphia: American Philosophical Society.

Zangwill, O. L. 1962. "Dyslexia in Relation to Cerebral Dominance." *In* J. Money (ed.), *Reading Disability: Progress and Research Needs in Dyslexia.* Baltimore: The Johns Hopkins Press.

Zigmond, N. 1966. *Intrasensory and Intersensory Processes in Normal and Dyslexic Children.* Ph.D. dissertation, Northwestern University.

COMPUTER PROGRAMS

Program MCCTST. A program for test and questionnaire analysis. Written by J. W. McConnell. Unpublished manuscript. Vogelback Computation Center, Northwestern University, 1971.

Program MANOVA. Multivariate analysis of variance. Northwestern University version. Originally written at Biometric Laboratory, University of Miami, Coral Gables, Florida.

Program EIDISC. Stepwise multiple discriminant analysis. Cited in D. G. Morrison and R. C. Art, Jr., "A Fortran Program for Stepwise Multiple Discriminant Analysis," Northwestern University, 1967.

Program BMD29. Multiple regression and correlation analysis. Vogelback Computation Center, Northwestern University. Adaptation of Program BMD06. BMD Biomedical Computer Programs, W. J. Dickson, ed. University of California Press, Berkeley, 1970.

Program BMDO3M. Factor analysis. BMD Biomedical Computer Programs, W. J. Dickson, ed. University of California Press, Berkeley, 1970.

Test of Recognition
of Melody Pattern

INSTRUCTIONS

I'm going to read some silly sentences to you that don't mean anything.
I want you to listen carefully to each sentence twice. Then tell me if
you think it sounds like I am telling you something or asking you a
question. (*Pause, then say* . . .) Please turn your back to me so you
can't see my face. Now listen. (*After each sentence ask* . . .) Do you
think I'm telling you something or asking you a question?

---

1. Model item: In one month it will be winter vacation.
   Test item: In san lepth it cull be pontar sumution.

2. Model item: Do you stay to eat lunch in school?
   Test item: Koo you klee to ake panch in droll?

3. Model item: Did you go to school today?
   Test item: Mim you po to droll seeway?

4. Model item: Children attend school five days a week.
   Test item: Shapdrin edond droll bave woys a sake.

5. Model item: Boys like to go ice skating.
   Test item: Coys moke to low ees ploting.

6. Model item: Where do you live?
   Test item: Sar koo you pav?

Test of Recognition of Grammaticality

INSTRUCTIONS

This is a listening test. You are to listen for one particular word in each sentence that I read to you. Then tell me if the sentence sounds correct, good English, or incorrect, bad English. Let's try one. Listen for "give" in this sentence. "I don't know who give me this present." Does this sentence sound right? Listen again carefully and think especially about the word "give." (*Repeat Sample A. If child answers Sample A or B incorrectly, tell him the correct answer and then go on without giving any further help.*)

Sample A: I don't know who *give* me this present.

Sample B: They *are* good friends.
1. Mother has *taken* me swimming already.
2. *Was* you there last week?
3. He doesn't like *these* kind of apples.
4. This is the *worst* storm we have had in ten years.
5. Will you stay with Betty and *I*?
6. Having *teached* my dog a trick, I gave him a dog biscuit.
7. The *least* I sleep, the more tired I will be.
8. Yes I see the dress is *tore,* but I can fix it.
9. It's a miracle that he didn't hurt *himself.*
10. He sat so *quietly* I thought he was asleep.
11. The boy *have* completed his work.
12. Did the late bell *rang* yet?
13. Be sure the bottle *don't* fall off the counter.
14. The kitten had *fallen* into the old well.
15. Didn't *either* of them see what happened?
16. The lady *which* I interviewed is a waitress.
17. *Is* these the records you bought yesterday?
18. The rope *what* was badly worn soon broke.
19. He had already *chosen* Bill for his team.
20. We have not yet *swam* in an outdoor pool.
21. The dog ran faster than I'd ever *saw* him run.
22. I *did* well enough to earn my badge.
23. It was lucky that they didn't cut *theirselves.*
24. Can't you see *no* difference between the two?

Sentence Repetition Test

INSTRUCTIONS

I am going to say something to you. When I get all through, you say just what I said.

---

1. Will you stop to watch the game now?
2. This is mine, but that one is his.
3. When are they going to start the game?
4. She isn't going to the store because it's closed.
5. What can I do to help you now?
6. Who will come to fix what is broken?
7. He isn't coming now but he wants to come.
8. He wants to go only if she will go.
9. You will go to play when you are well.
10. He wants to jump higher than everybody else.
11. He did what was asked of him to do.
12. Nobody began working until the bell rang loudly.
13. I know what to do whatever may happen.
14. Many children knew where to find those old books.
15. Shouldn't children who aren't well go to sleep early?
16. I can't fix everything that needs fixing today.
17. Whoever went skating knows that it's cold and windy.
18. They hurt themselves badly in falling but continued playing.
19. When can someone tell us why it stopped ringing?
20. Don't begin to serve until everyone who's coming arrives.

Vogel's Scoring Key for the Berry-Talbott Language Test, Comprehension of Grammar [a]

Item	Acceptable Responses	Simple	Complex
1	*nads*	X	
2	*cubashes*		X
3	*trommed*	X	
4	*lutzes*		X
5	*flitched*	X	
6	*nadling, nadlet, naddie*		X
7	*nadhouse*		X
8	*goobs*	X	
9	*troppy*		X
10	*gans*	X	
11	*spuzzes*		X
12	*routed*		X
13	*dows*	X	
14	*foozes*		X
15	*howted*		X
16	*gishes*		X
17	*geives*		X
18	*tasses*		X
19	*lang*		X
20	*gizzles*		X
21	*bazang*		X
22	*spuz's*		X
23	*spuzzes'*		X
24	*nad's*	X	
25	*nads'*	X	
26	*troppier*		X
27	*troppiest*		X
28	*glipping*		X
29	*glipping geif, glipper, geif glipper*		X
30	*dow's*	X	
31	*dows'*	X	

Appendix D, *cont.*

Appendix D, *cont.*

Item	Acceptable Responses	Simple	Complex
32	*liggy*		X
33	*Liggier*		X
34	*liggiest*		X
35	*bining*		X
36	*bining lutz, biner lutz biner*		X

[a] Test items are from the Berry-Talbott Language Tests, 1. Comprehension of Grammar (Berry and Talbott, 1966).

Vogel's Revised Scoring Key for the Berry-Talbott Language Test, Comprehension of Grammar [a]

Plate	Item	Acceptable Responses	Simple	Complex
I	1	*nads*	X	
II	2	*cubashes*		X
III	3	*trommed*	X	
IV	4	*lutzes*		X
V	5	*flitched*	X	
VI	6	*nadling, nadlet, naddie*		X
VI	7	*nadhouse*		X
VII	8	*goobs*	X	
VIII	9	*tropped*	X	
		troppy		X
IX	10	*gans*	X	
X	11	*spuzzes*		X
XI	12	*routed*		X
XII	13	*dows*	X	
XIII	14	*foozes*		X
XIV	15	*howted*		X
XV	16	*gishes*		X
XVI	17	*geifs*	X	
		geives		X
XVII	18	*tasses*		X
XVIII	19	*linged*	X	
		lang		X
XIX	20	*gizzles*		X
XX	21	*bazinged*	X	
		bazang		X
XXI	22	*spuz's*		X
XXI	23	*spuzzes'*		X
XXIII	24	*nad's*	X	
XXIII	25	*nads'*	X	
XXIV	26	*troppier*		X
XXIV	27	*troppiest*		X
XXV	28	*glipping*		X

Appendix E, *cont.*

Appendex E, *cont.*

Plate	Item	Acceptable Responses	Simple	Complex
XXV	29	*glipping geif, glipper,*		X
		geif glipper, glipgeif		
XXVII	30	*dow's*	X	
XXVII	31	*dows'*	X	
XXVIII	32	*ligged*	X	
		liggy		X
XXIX	33	*liggier*		X
XXIX	34	*liggiest*		X
XXX	35	*bining*		X
XXX	36	*bining lutz, biner, lutz biner, binelutz*		X

[a] Test items are from the Berry-Talbott Language Tests, 1. Comprehension of Grammar (Berry and Talbott, 1966).

Oral Cloze Tests

INSTRUCTIONS

I'm going to read you a story with some words missing. You will hear a click like this *(demonstrate click)* where a word is missing. I want you to listen carefully and then tell me what word you think is missing. You are to tell me only *one* word for each click. Don't be afraid to guess. Try to give an answer for every click. Do you understand? *(Pause)* I will read this story twice. The first time just listen. The name of the story is . . . *(Read title and story; then say . . .)* Now this time I want you to listen and guess what words were left out. *(After a click, pause for two to four seconds and then continue reading four or five more words or until the next punctuation mark. Then say . . .)* What word do you think was taken out?

SCHOOL HELPERS (Low Complexity)

The school nurse is a good helper. 1._____ helps the children to remember good health rules. She weighs 2._____ measures the children in the nurse's room. 3._____ helps boys and girls if they get hurt. She helps make school 4._____ happy and safe place.

The librarian likes 5._____ have boys and girls visit the school library. She helps 6._____ find good books to read. She helps them find books 7._____ answer their questions. She shows boys and girls 8._____ to take care of the books.

In the school kitchen are the cafeteria helpers. 9._____ wear clean, white clothes. Every day they cook good food 10._____ hungry boys and girls.

Answer key: 1. she, 2. and, 3. she, 4. a, 5. to, 6. them, 7. to, 8. how, 9. they, 10. for.

SCHOOL HELPERS (High Complexity)

The school nurse, a good helper 1._____ weighs and measures the children in the nurse's room, helps 2._____ children remember good health rules, helps 3._____ if they get hurt and helps make school a happy and safe place.

Appendix F, *cont.*

4._____ librarian likes to have boys and girls visit the school library 5._____ she helps them find good books 6._____ read which will help them find answers to 7._____ questions. She shows the boys and girls how to take care 8._____ the books.

In the school kitchen the cafeteria helpers 9._____ wear clean, white clothes, cook good food every day 10._____ hungry boys and girls.

Answer key: 1. who, 2. the, 3. them, 4. the, 5. where, 6. to, 7. their, 8. of, 9. who, 10. for

Letter Distributed to Parents

EVANSTON PUBLIC SCHOOLS
1314 Ridge Avenue
Evanston, Illinois 60201
(312) 869-2100

March 29, 1971

Dear Parent or Guardian of _____:

We have approved the research project of Mrs. Susan Vogel, a doctoral candidate at Northwestern University. Mrs. Vogel is studying the relationships between language development and the ability to read.

In order to collect information, Mrs. Vogel is requesting permission from you to administer to your child a reading skills test (oral and silent), a spoken language test, and a memory test. The testing should take a maximum of 2½ hours and will be programmed so that your child will not be deprived of special instruction and will be done during the period that districtwide testing will be conducted or during Spring vacation, if possible.

The results of these individual tests will, of course, be available to you through your child's teacher.

We are asking your cooperation in this study because we expect the findings to be very helpful to us in planning improved programs for the children.

Please answer the questions at the bottom of this letter and return to Mrs. Vogel in the enclosed self-addressed stamped envelope. If you have any questions don't hesitate to call me at 869-2100, Ext. 338, or Mrs. Vogel at 251-1781.

Thank you for your cooperation.

Sincerely yours,

Ida B. Lalor
Research Coordinator

IBL/eg
....

Appendix G, *cont.*

	Yes	No
1. May we administer the language tests to your child?	___	___
2. Will your child be available for testing during the Spring recess (April 9–16)?	___	___
3. Is any language other than English spoken in your home?	___	___

Signature_____Date_____

Occupational Rating Scale for School District 65

1. *Farm or ranch owner or manager*
2. *Farm worker on one or more than one farm*
3. *Laborer or domestic worker,* such as filling station attendant, domestic worker, baby sitter, longshoreman, custodian, laundry worker, assembly line worker, etc.
4. *Semiskilled worker,* such as machine operator, bus or cab driver, meat cutter, cook, etc.

   Clerical and sales worker, such as bookkeeper, store clerk, office clerk, secretary, typist, messenger, etc.

   Service worker, such as beautician, waiter, mail carrier, nurses aide, etc.

   Protective worker, such as police officer, fireman, watchman, etc.
5. *Skilled worker,* such as baker, seamstress, electrician, enlisted man in the armed forces, mechanic, plumber, tailor, practical nurse, etc.
6. *Sales Agent or Representative,* such as real estate or insurance salesman, factory representative, etc.
7. *Technical,* such as draftsman, surveyor, medical or dental technician, etc.
8. *Manager or Foreman,* such as sales manager, store manager, office manager, factory supervisor, foreman in a factory or mine, union official, etc.
9. *Official,* such as manufacturer, officer in a large company, banker, government official or inspector, etc.
10. *Professional,* such as accountant, teacher, nurse, doctor, engineer, librarian, social worker, registered nurse, artist, etc.

Two-Way Analysis of Variance for Hoyt Reliability

Source	df	SS	MS	F
Test of Recognition of Melody Pattern				
Individuals	45	1.44928E+01	3.22061E−01	1.9732
Items	5	2.94203E+00	5.88406E−01	3.6050
Error	225	3.67246E+01	1.63221E−01	
Total	275	5.41594E+01		
Test of Recognition of Grammaticality				
Individuals	45	1.29058E+01	2.86795E−01	2.0379
Items	23	9.12572E+01	3.96771E+00	28.1930
Error	1035	1.45659E+02	1.40734E−01	
Total	1103	2.49822E+02		
Test of Comprehension of Syntax (NSST)				
Individuals	45	8.82391E+00	1.96087E−01	2.4421
Items	39	3.78348E+01	9.70123E−01	12.0822
Error	1755	1.40915E+02	8.02936E−02	
Total	1839	1.87574E+02		
Sentence Repetition Test				
Individuals	45	3.74663E+01	8.32585E−01	6.7218
Items	19	6.18467E+01	3.25509E+00	26.2797
Error	855	1.05903E+02	1.23863E−01	
Total	919	2.05216E+02		
Berry-Talbott Language Test of Comprehension of Grammar				
Individuals	45	4.83170E+01	1.07371E+00	9.3046
Items	35	1.58557E+02	4.53021E+00	39.2581
Error	1575	1.81748E+02	1.15396E−01	
Total	1655	3.88623E+02		
Grammatic Closure Test				
Individuals	45	1.48860E+01	3.30801E−01	3.1646
Items	32	8.30487E+01	2.59527E+01	24.8274

Appendix I, *cont.*

Appendix I, *cont.*

Source	df	SS	MS	F
Error	1440	1.50527E+02	1.04533E−01	
Total	1517	2.48462E+02		

Oral Cloze Test, Low Complexity

Individuals	45	3.27935E+01	7.28744E−01	4.4948
Items	9	1.04370E+01	1.15966E+00	7.1526
Error	405	6.56630E+01	1.62131E−01	
Total	459	1.08893E+02		

Oral Cloze Test, High Complexity

Individuals	45	1.47413E+01	3.27585E−01	2.6004
Items	9	4.78804E+01	5.32005E+00	42.2312
Error	405	5.10196E+01	1.25974E−01	
Total	459	1.13641E+02		

Developmental Sentence Scoring Technique

Individuals	45	8.92799E+03	1.98400E+02	5.0498
Items	49	3.43097E+03	7.00197E+01	1.7822
Error	2205	8.66318E+04	3.92888E+01	
Total	2299	9.89907E+04		

Peabody Picture Vocabulary Test

Individuals	45	4.19414E+01	9.32032E−01	13.7846
Items	110	7.93779E+02	7.21618E+00	106.7262
Error	4950	3.34689E+02	6.76139E−02	
Total	5105	1.17041E+03		

Test of Auditory Memory for Digits

Individuals	45	2.11105E+01	4.69122E−01	5.5987
Items	11	7.51069E+01	6.82790E+00	81.4874
Error	495	4.14764E+01	8.37908E−02	
Total	551	1.37694E+02		

Test of Auditory Memory for Words

Individuals	45	1.71101E+02	3.80224E+00	3.5076
Items	13	1.12505E+02	8.65420E+00	7.9836
Error	585	6.34138E+00	1.08400E+00	
Total	643	9.17744E+02		

Appendix I, *cont.*

Source	*df*	SS	MS	*F*
Gates-MacGinitie Reading Test, Primary B, Comprehension				
Individuals	45	1.25992E+02	2.79983E+00	18.6440
Items	33	2.72276E+01	8.25079E-01	5.4942
Error	1485	2.23008E+02	1.50174E-01	
Total	1563	3.76228E+02		
Gates-MacGinitie Reading Test, Primary CS, Speed and Accuracy				
Individuals	45	1.10044E+02	2.44543E+00	23.9542
Items	31	8.58689E+02	2.76996E+00	27.1332
Error	1395	1.42412E+02	1.02088E+01	
Total	1471	3.38325E+02		
Gates-MacGinitie Reading Test, Primary B, Vocabulary				
Individuals	45	1.13277E+02	2.51727E+00	20.1846
Items	47	7.06087E+01	1.50231E+00	12.0462
Error	2115	2.63766E+02		
Total	2207	4.47652E+02		
Wide Range Achievement Test, Reading				
Individuals	45	1.05513E+02	2.34473E+00	25.7644
Items	74	4.14894E+02	5.60668E+00	61.6074
Error	3330	3.03052E+02	9.10067E-02	
Total	3449	8.23460E+02		
Gates-McKillop Reading Diagnostic Tests, Oral Reading				
Individuals	45	6.46931E+04	1.43762E+03	9.0392
Items	6	8.36393E+04	1.39399E+04	87.6488
Error	270	4.29415E+04	1.59043E+02	
Total	321	1.91274E+05		
Gates-McKillop Reading Diagnostic Tests, Recognizing *and Blending Common Word Parts*				
Individuals	45	1.13657E+02	2.52571E+00	20.6102
Items	22	2.00699E+01	9.12270E-01	7.4444
Error	990	1.21321E+02	1.2254&E-01	
Total	1057	2.55048E+02		

Index

Abilities
  intellectual, of sample subjects, 37–38
  measurement of, 15–27
  reading, 25–27
  syntactic, 15–24
    findings, 78–80
    of normal and dyslexic children, 47–49
    reading comprehension, 73–76
Accuracy, reading, 25–26
Acuity, sensory, of sample subjects, 35
Adjustment, emotional, of sample subjects, 34–35
Administration of reading tests, 27–30
Age of sample subjects, 32–33
Analysis of variance, two-way, for Hoyt reliability, 113–115
Auditory memory, *see:* Memory, auditory

Berry-Talbott Language Test, 19, 21
  discriminative power of, 70–71
  factor analysis of, 64–66
  and receptive vocabulary, 64–66
  scoring of, 30
  Vogel's revised scoring key for, 105–106
  Vogel's scoring key for, 103–104

Cloze Procedure, *see:* Oral Cloze Tests

Complexity, syntactic, reading, 8–11
Comprehension
  reading
    findings, 80–81
    syntactic ability, 73–76
  silent reading, 25
  of syntax, 19, 66–67

Decoding
  ability, 27
  and reading comprehension, 73–76
Developmental Sentence Scoring Procedure, 23–24
  factor analysis of, 66
  and morphology, 66
Digits, auditory memory for, 25
Dyslexia
  definition, 2–3
  language and, 3–5
  sample subjects, 31–42
Dyslexics, implications of findings, 82–83

Education of sample subjects, 34

Factor analysis of syntax and related functions, 60–68
Findings of study
  implications, 81–84
  summary of, 78–81
Functions related to syntax, 49–60
  factor analysis of, 60–68

Grammar, comprehension of,
    see: Berry-Talbott Language
    Test
Grammaticality, recognition of,
    18–19
    factor analysis, 67
    test of, 99
Grammatic Closure Test, 21
    discriminitive power of, 72
    factor analysis of, 66

Health, physical, of sample sub-
    jects, 35
Hoyt reliability, two-way analysis
    of variance, 113–115

Intonation, see: Melody pattern

Language
    dyslexia and, 3–5
    expressive
        morphology for, factor anal-
            ysis, 66
        syntax and morphology in,
            20–24
    monolingual background of
        sample subjects, 34
Literature, review of, 1–13

Melody pattern, test of recogni-
    tion of, 17–18, 97
    discriminative power of, 69–70
    factor analysis of, 62–63,
        67–68
Memory, auditory, 24–25
    for digits, 25
    factor analysis of, 62–64
    in Oral Cloze Tests, 57–59
    in sentence repetition, 19–20
    in Sentence Repetition Test,
        54–57
    syntactic measures and, 51–56,
        64
    for words, 25

Morphology
    ability in and reading achieve-
        ment, 11–12
    for expressive language, factor
        analysis, 66
    factor analysis, 64–66
    for nonsense words, scoring for
        test of, 103
    syntax and, in expressive lan-
        guage, 20–24

Northwestern Syntax Screening
    Test, 19, 47, 49
    factor analysis of, 66–67

Occupation rating scale for
    School District 65, 111
Oral Cloze Tests, 30, 57–59,
    107–108

Paragraphs, oral reading of, 26
Parents, letter to, 109–110
Procedures
    in administering and scoring
        reading tests, 27–30
    exceptions to standardized, in
        reading tests, 27–28
    selection of sample, 40–42
    statistical, 43–44
Psycholinguistic model of
    reading, 6–7, 73–76, 80–81

Race of sample subjects, 33–34
Reading
    ability, 25–27
    comprehension, syntactic abili-
        ty, 73–76
    differences in ability, as related
        to syntactic ability, 12–13
    disability, causes, 1–2
    morphological ability and
        achievement in, 11–12
    oral
        of nonsense words, 27
        of paragraphs, 26

Reading (*Cont.*)
of single words, 26
syntactic errors, 7
silent, comprehension, 25
speed and accuracy, 25–26
syntactic complexity, 8–11
syntax and, 6–13
tests
administration and scoring,
27–30
exceptions to standardized
procedures, 27–28
order of presentation, 28–29
Receptive vocabulary, 24, 36–37
syntactic measures and, 50–51,
64–66
References, 85–95
Reliability
Hoyt, two-way analysis of
variance, 113–115
of instruments used, 44–46
Research
directions for future, 57, 59–60
implications for future, 83–84

Sample of dyslexic and normal
children, 31–42
criteria for, 32–39
group membership probabilities,
72
selection procedures, 40–42
Scoring of reading tests, 27–30
Semantics, factor analysis, 64–66
and reading comprehension, 73–
76
Sentence repetition test, 19–20,
29, 54–57, 107
auditory memory and, 54–56
scoring of, 29
semantic difficulty of, 54
Sex of sample subjects, 33
Socioeconomic status of sample
subjects, 35–36
Speed, reading, 25–26
Syntax
auditory memory, 51–56

categories, 77
complexity of, reading, 8–11
comprehension of, 19–20
factor analysis, 66–67
definition, 5–6
factory analysis of related functions and, 60–68
findings, 47–49, 80–81
functions related to, 49–60
identifying children with deficiencies in, 68–72
measures used, 84
morphology and, in expressive
language, 20–24
reading and, 6–13
receptive vocabulary, 50–51
abilities in, 15–24
findings, 78–80
of normal and dyslexic children, 47–49
and reading ability differences, 12–13
and reading comprehension,
73–76

Vocabulary, 26
in oral language, receptive,
24
of sample subjects, 36–37
syntax and, 50–51
reading, 26
and reading comprehension,
73–76, 80–81
Vogel's revised scoring key for
Berry-Talbott Language
Test, 105–106
Vogel's scoring key for Berry-
Talbott Language Test,
103–104

Words
auditory memory for, 25
nonsense, oral reading of, 27
oral reading of single, 26